Praise for *Theol*

"This book offers a needed pol
ecological devastation we urgen

out an intersectional analysis of ecological issues, we are lost. Rethinking the work of theology for the planet's sustainability and flourishing is this book's great achievement."

—Keri Day, Princeton Theological Seminary

"Joerg Rieger has long and persuasively brought theology to bear upon the power of class. Now he binds his challenge to global capitalism with the full-bodied complexity of gender, sex, and race. And most importantly, he embeds this transnational intersectionalism in the precarious vibrancy of the earth. What can be more important—for all of us working earthlings—than his eco-social theology of *deep solidarity*?"
—Catherine Keller, George T. Cobb Professor of Constructive Theology, Drew University Theological School

"Rieger provides trenchant analysis of the stark power differentials inherent in neoliberal capitalism that enable a few to maximize profit at terrible expense to the many and to Earth's ecosystems. In response he calls for a 'deep solidarity' based on the labor and collective agency of working-class people. Of tremendous value are his insistence that privilege does not always equal power, his locating the roots of climate change in the structures of capitalism as a way of life, and his honest inquiry into the roles of theology in either maintaining or undermining oppressive power. This text deftly weaves stark critique together with pragmatic and visionary possibility."
—Cynthia Moe-Lobeda, professor of theological and social ethics, Pacific Lutheran Theological Seminary of California Lutheran University, and Church Divinity School of the Pacific; director, PLTS Center for Climate Justice and Faith; core doctoral faculty, Graduate Theological Union

"*Theology in the Capitalocene* is an extraordinary proposal for deep solidarities beyond reductionism. Drawing from a true diversity of voices from disenfranchised communities, Joerg Rieger superbly connects the study of economics, religion, and ecology, effectively unmasking and breaking universalized ideological hegemonies. By doing so he opens novel paths for confronting both capitalist catastrophes and capitalist narratives of catastrophes in the twenty-first century. This is a must-read for anyone interested in political theologies, liberation practices, radical social movements, race and religion, and the most current social and political theories."

—Santiago Slabodsky, the Robert and Florence Kaufman Endowed Chair in Jewish Studies, and associate professor of religion, Hofstra University

"This book is a powerful and persuasive theology of catastrophe and solidarity that yields a genuine and mature hope in the face of a commodified globe and racialized capitalism. Joerg Rieger is keeping alive a great prophetic tradition!"

—Cornel West, Union Theological Seminary

"Rieger offers a generative exploration of deep solidarity that 'deploys diversity rather than uniformity' and 'brings together the many to stand up for themselves.' Consistently dissatisfied with simplistic framings, he centers labor and class relationships, their significance for Christian theology, and how they matter for rethinking intersectionally about planetary thriving."

—Traci C. West, author of *Solidarity and Defiant Spirituality: Africana Lessons on Racism, Religion, and Ending Gender Violence*

Dispatches: Turning Points in Theology and Global Crises

Dispatches: Turning Points in Theology and Global Crises draws on the legacy of early twentieth-century theological responses to the crises of the two world wars. During World War II, the Signposts series (Dacre Press, 1940) sought to offer an interruption of a theological malaise in the midst of mass violence and destruction. Contributors from that series, including Julian Casserley, Eric Mascall, and Donald MacKinnon, among others, offered slim volumes that drew from diverse resources and harnessed the apocalyptic political urgency of the dialectical school within the theological grammar of a more traditional Anglo-Catholic Thomism. Similarly, and inspired significantly by MacKinnon's contributions, this present series draws on diverse theological resources in order to offer urgent responses to contemporary crises.

While the title of the series conveys the digest nature of the volumes, the subtitle, Turning Points, indicates the apocalyptic urgency of the issues addressed and yet reserves any prescriptive judgment on the manner in which the tradition can be reappropriated by our authors. In this way, we seek to offer a genuinely creative and disruptive theological-ethical *ressourcement* for church in the present moment. With conceptual agility and faithfulness, this series will provide intelligent and yet accessible reflections on the shape and form of theological life in the present.

Dispatches will illuminate and explore, creatively and concisely, the implications and relevance of theology for the global crises of late modernity. Our authors have been invited to introduce succinct and provocative arguments intended to provoke dialogue and exchange of ideas while setting in relief the implications of theology for political and moral life.

Series Editors

Ashley John Moyse (PhD, Newcastle) is the McDonald Postdoctoral Fellow in Christian Ethics and Public Life, Christ Church, University of Oxford. In addition to his work with the Dispatches series, he is the author of *Reading Karl Barth, Interrupting Moral Technique, Transforming Biomedical Ethics* (Palgrave, 2015) and *The Art of Living for a Technological Age* (Fortress, 2021). He has also coedited several volumes, including *Correlating Sobornost: Conversations between Karl Barth and the Russian Orthodox Tradition* (Fortress, 2016), *Kenotic Ecclesiology: Select Writings of Donald M. MacKinnon* (Fortress, 2016), and *Treating the Body in Medicine and Religion: Jewish, Christian, and Islamic Perspectives* (Routledge, 2019).

Scott A. Kirkland (PhD, Newcastle) is the John and Jeane Stockdale Lecturer in Practical Theology and Ethics and research coordinator for the Trinity College Theological School, University of Divinity, Melbourne. He is the author of *Into the Far Country: Karl Barth and the Modern Subject* (Fortress, 2016); coauthor, with John C. McDowell, of *Eschatology* (Eerdmans, 2018); and coeditor, with Ashley John Moyse and John C. McDowell, of *Correlating Sobornost: Conversations between Karl Barth and the Russian Orthodox Tradition* (Fortress, 2016) and *Kenotic Ecclesiology: Select Writings of Donald M. MacKinnon* (Fortress, 2016).

Published Titles

The End Is Not Yet by John W. de Gruchy
Political Orthodoxies by Cyril Hovorun
Theology and the Globalized Present by John C. McDowell
Theology, Comedy, Politics by Marcus Pound
The Art of Living for a Technological Age by Ashley John Moyse
Theology in the Capitalocene by Joerg Rieger

Theology in the Capitalocene

Theology in the Capitalocene

Capitalocene

Ecology, Identity, Class, and Solidarity

Joerg Rieger

Fortress Press
Minneapolis

*To those yearning for the liberation of
people, planet, and the divine*

Contents

Introduction

Troubling Intersections in the Capitalocene

The Intersections of Theology

In times of rising pressures and catastrophe, people yearn for alternatives. So does the planet. Protests are often a start, bubbling up from growing unease and discomfort with what is. But the success of protests depends on being able to make oneself heard and on political, economic, cultural, or religious power. And without the parallel production of political, economic, cultural, and religious alternatives, even protests tend to get stuck in the imagination of the dominant systems, often without knowing it. Rebellion is not revolution, nor does it always lead to transformation.

This book is dedicated to a closer look at what causes unease and discomfort in our time, leading to the growing destruction and death of people and the planet. Only when the causes are addressed in depth can real alternatives be developed, which is the goal of this text. But for alternatives to be real and measure up to the size of the challenge, all hands need to be on deck. This is the reason why I keep coming back to the touchy topic of solidarity—which is the biggest nightmare of the dominant systems—and why this work can only be done at the seemingly impossible intersections of everything. This is the location of theology in the Capitalocene—the geological age when the maximization of economic profit has made it to the center stage not only in the United States but all over the globe and dominates whatever other ages have been proclaimed, including the Anthropocene and what one scholar has called the "Chthulucene."[1] Theology in the Capitalocene starts with an account of the dominant powers in order to identify alternatives, and it needs to be both local and global and always international, incorporating the intersections of human and nonhuman developments.

For some time now, political and public theologies have gained currency. These developments are significant, as everything is ultimately political and public, even that which at first sight seems personal and private. The personal is political, as feminist thinkers have reminded us, and we should add that the political is also personal. At the same time, politics may well be playing sandbox games or rearranging the chairs on the *Titanic* without economic analysis, if it is true that we find ourselves not in the geological age of the Anthropocene, when humanity as a whole asserts its

---

1   Philosopher Donna Haraway has proposed the notion of the Chthulucene, when agency includes "ongoing multispecies stories and practices of becoming-with." This concept is powerful, but it is more aspirational than analytical of current constellations of power; Donna Haraway, "Tentacular Thinking: Anthropocene, Capitalocene, and Chthulucene," *e-flux Journal*, no. 75 (September 2016), https://www.e-flux.com/journal/75/67125/tentacular-thinking-anthropocene-capitalocene-chthulucene/. For the concept of the Capitalocene, see Jason W. Moore, "Anthropocene or Capitalocene? Nature, History, and the Crisis of Capitalism," in *Anthropocene or Capitalocene? Nature, History, and the Crisis of Capitalism*, ed. Jason W. Moore (Oakland, CA: PM, 2016), 1–12.

power over everything, but in the age of the Capitalocene, when the economic interests of a small and privileged group of humans rule both people and the planet. The study of theology and religion can be helpful here, since both politics and economics at times resemble religions that worship the status quo.[2] In other words, there are connections among politics, economics, and religion that must be accounted for by theology in the Capitalocene. Theology can no longer limit itself to the religious, but neither can it limit itself to religion and politics without considering the economic flows of power in a global context.

The classic triad of gender, race, and class marks the place where all hands on deck are needed in theological efforts in the Capitalocene. Today, this triad must be broadened to include concerns along the lines of ethnicity, sexuality, nationality, and ecology. The horizon is determined not primarily by individual experiences and identities but by global structures of exploitation, extraction, and oppression. In order to produce real alternatives, all of these elements need to be made to work together in complex interactions—simply adding them up will not do, as multifaceted power is messy. Without solidarities that match this complexity and messiness, the best we can hope for is individual forms of inclusion into the dominant system and some recognition of diversity, which may be preferable to exclusion and forced homogeneity but will hardly lead to systemic change and liberation.

---

2 Walter Benjamin went one step further, arguing that Christianity since the Reformation has not only supported the rise of capitalism but become identical to it; Walter Benjamin, *Kapitalismus Als Religion*, ed. Dirk Baecker, 2nd ed. (Berlin: Kulturverlag Kadmos, 2004), 17.

The good, and perhaps somewhat surprising, news is that places exist where all hands are already on deck, even if only by default—for instance, in places where the global 99 percent have to work for a living. This is why theology in the Capitalocene needs to engage questions of work and productive and reproductive labor (including their limits, lack, and liberation)—topics that theologians at present rarely address. Almost everything (including matters of identity and class) comes together in places of work, whether these places are formal, informal, or currently invisible. All hands are currently on deck, especially in those parts of the workforce branded as "essential" in the wake of the Covid-19 pandemic. And while the working class in the United States was never merely white men in blue overalls or hard hats, today this working class is among the most diverse and international in the world. Women; racial, ethnic, and sexual minorities; Indigenous people; and generations of immigrants all find themselves working together in efforts of production and reproduction. Unemployed, underemployed, casually employed, and no-longer-employed people are also part of this working class as well, as we shall see in chapter 3. This diversity is increasingly reflected in the makeup of labor unions as well.[3] Unfortunately, religious communities and even political endeavors often still lag behind, even though things are beginning to change there as well. And while places of work and labor are designed to employ diversity in the production and reproduction of the dominant status quo, they

---

3 Kayla Blado, Dan Essrow, and Lawrence Mishel, "Who Are Today's Union Members?," Economic Policy Institute, August 31, 2017, https://www.epi.org/publication/who-are-todays-union-members/.

are also some of the most significant places for inspiration for resistance and the production of alternative power to emerge.

All "hands" are on deck, finally, also when it comes to the nonhuman environment, even though here the metaphor breaks down. Theology in the Capitalocene needs to take into account that collaboration is real in the incredible diversity of the nonhuman world and its productive dynamics, which humans are still discovering.[4] This collaboration is under attack by capitalist exploitation and extraction, which is causing unprecedented loss of nonhuman agency and biodiversity and affects even those parts of the natural world that humans have not yet explored, like organisms in the depths of the oceans or the recesses of the human body.[5] The most adventurous capitalists are already preparing for the exploitation of the cosmos and the extraction of its resources, beyond planet Earth, symbolic of the realities at the heart of the Capitalocene.[6] But in the nonhuman world, too, resistance emerges, as we will see.

The circle closes when it becomes clear that the exploitation and extraction of planetary resources parallel the exploitation and extraction of human labor. For good or for ill, human productive and reproductive labor and nonhuman reproductive labor are more closely related than many realize

---

4   Gabriel Popkin, "'Wood Wide Web'—the Underground Network of Microbes That Connects Trees—Mapped for First Time," Science, May 15, 2019, https://www.science.org/content/article/wood-wide-web-underground-network-microbes-connects-trees-mapped-first-time.

5   "UN Report: Nature's Dangerous Decline 'Unprecedented'; Species Extinction Rates 'Accelerating,'" United Nations, May 6, 2019, https://www.un.org/sustainabledevelopment/blog/2019/05/nature-decline-unprecedented-report/.

6   The three most prominent individuals are Jeff Bezos, Sir Richard Branson, and Elon Musk.

(Karl Marx, using the outdated binary language of his time, talked about nature as the mother and labor as the father of wealth; see chapter 1). And no life would exist without reproductive labor in the broadest sense—this is truly a matter of life and death, being and nonbeing, tied to the deepest theological themes as well as the cores of politics and economics. This is why, at the very core of the argument of this book, productive and reproductive labor will be discussed in terms of Paul Tillich's notion of the "ultimate concern" and Friedrich Schleiermacher's concept of "absolute dependence" in chapter 3.

What is still mostly unexplored is how the labor of non-human nature—all of it—is contributing to the alternatives and the transformation we are looking for. Theology in the Capitalocene needs to engage these matters, and some work is already being done on this topic (see chapter 2), although this book can only scratch the surface of this question.

In any case, what does not work—now or ever—is individualism. Contrary to common belief, individualism is an illusion that is simply not an option in a world that is as interconnected as ours. The myths of individualism and of individual solutions amount to cover-ups of existing relationships, and even protests of individualism often make things worse if they assume that individualism is a real option. To give some examples, the carbon-footprint calculators that many well-meaning people use were invented by British Petroleum (BP) to cover up its role in climate change, which is why the fossil fuel industry continues to promote them.[7]

---

7   Rebecca Solnit, "Big Oil Coined 'Carbon Footprints' to Blame Us for Their Greed: Keep Them on the Hook," *Guardian*, August 23, 2021, https://www.theguardian.com/

Another example is the notion that hard work makes billionaires, as it covers up the fact that large fortunes can only be built with the help and on the back of others. Contrary to the fantasy of the American Dream, billionaires are not models of rugged individualism but the product of myriads of connections that are forged to work in their favor. The same could be said of collectives that appear to be acting like individuals, like tight-knit religious communities or certain identity groups: no one and no group is ever self-made, all are always shaped by larger relationships (for good and for ill), and no substantial transformation of anything can happen without acknowledging the fact that individualism is the myth of the powerful and privileged rather than the reality. As a result, any real solution, whether economic, political, or religious, will need to engage structural relationships at every level and take into account the flows of power.

The Work of Theology

For a long time, theology seemed most at home in the proverbial ivory towers of the academy, where its influence once used to be considerable. Whenever theology ventured outside of the academy, it often linked up with another set of ivory towers, symbolized by church steeples. There, too, it used to have some influence. As both the academy and the church made efforts to escape from their respective ivory towers—often by making common cause with business ventures,

---

commentisfree/2021/aug/23/big-oil-coined-carbon-footprints-to-blame-us-for-their -greed-keep-them-on-the-hook.

corporations, and politics—theology has tried to join, lagging behind in many cases. But rebellion against ivory towers is not revolution, even if it is directed against traditional Eurocentric (or Americentric) ideals. Nor does this kind of rebellion necessarily lead to transformation.

Contrary to common belief, none of these ivory towers ever existed in isolation in the first place. Actual and metaphoric academic and ecclesial ivory towers were built at great expense, meaning that they were at no time removed from economics and politics. Over time, the maintenance of these ivory towers requires substantial efforts; it seems that increased support is needed the older and more established they get. Questions like who funds and has an interest in maintaining these institutions and who pays for the salaries of construction workers, architects, and janitors, who build and maintain actual towers, and professors, pastors, and administrators, who maintain their metaphorical equivalents, provide some insights. Questions of funding and interest allow for a peek not only into political and economic dynamics but also into the intellectual and theological issues negotiated in academy and church.

This short reflection on ivory towers matches Antonio Gramsci's notion of "traditional intellectuals."[8] These intellectuals mistakenly assumed that they were doing their academic work in autonomous and independent fashion—as if in ivory towers—and categorically ignored questions of how their work might be related to economics, politics, and power.

---

8 Antonio Gramsci, *Selections from the Prison Notebooks*, ed. and trans. Quintin Hoare and Geoffrey Nowell Smith (New York: International, 1971), 233.

By ignoring these questions, the academic work of traditional intellectuals unintentionally supported the economic and political power structures of their time and propped up the dominant status quo. While Gramsci was talking about the intellectuals of his time, including Roman Catholic theologians and clergy, it seems that something like this has been going on ever since aloof intellectuals first emerged in universities and the church, and it continues today.

Aware of these problems, theology in the Capitalocene can benefit from taking a leaf from Gramsci's notion of the organic intellectual, which he developed in contrast to his critique of traditional intellectuals.[9] At first sight, it may look like what is now called contextual theology has embraced the ethos of Gramsci's notion of organic intellectuals, but important aspects of the conversation are often still missing. Even though contextual theologies remedy the neglect of context that marked the work of Gramsci's traditional intellectuals, they are often developed as if they addressed matters of special interest. This is reflected, for instance, in certain debates about cultural appropriation, which are conducted as if context were a matter of ownership so that male theologians should not present the insights of female theologians, white theologians should not present the insights of Black theologians, and so on. To be sure, cultural appropriation can be problematic and part of a colonizing mindset when presenting the insights of others without awareness of existing relationships (traditional and way-too-narrow definitions of male and female as well as Black and white, for

---

9   Gramsci, 3–23. Liberation theologies occasionally picked up this term as well.

instance, are never independent of each other) and when differentials of power are ignored. But thinking about contexts along the lines of property ownership can prevent cross-fertilization, constructive engagement, and transformation.

For Gramsci, the concept of the organic intellectual was based on a recognition of hegemony and class and on the need for taking sides with the many—a rather diverse group in his native Italy—rather than the few. Building on this insight, organic theologians deal with matters of context not primarily in terms of the uniqueness of individual contexts but in terms of a hegemonic relationship of contexts, permeated by the flow of power. For organic theologians, the question of context, therefore, is not about "lifting up" specific minority contexts (for instance, with the intent of including them into the dominant system), nor is it about volunteering their time "for any enterprise (even the most bizarre) which is vaguely subversive."[10] Rather, the question of context is about locating hegemony and power differentials with an eye toward liberation. Organic theologians engage context with an awareness of where the conflicts are and where they themselves are located in relation to the dominant powers, realizing that they are rarely benefiting as much from these powers as they are led to believe. This is why class analysis is so crucial, in conjunction with analyses of gender, sexuality, race, ethnicity, nationality, and so on. Based on this analysis, organic theologians take sides and operate in solidarity because they know that power differentials are never random but tend to work in concert to serve the exploitation

---

10   Gramsci, 203. Gramsci also challenges "false heroisms" (204).

of the many by the few. Organic theologians know that the various power differentials can only be overcome when the many pull together in order to counter the efforts of the few who rule supreme, and they are not afraid to ask questions about the location of the divine in all of this.

To be sure, organic theologians today may find themselves in even more complex situations than the organic intellectuals of Gramsci's time, and solidarity has become a more complex challenge as well. As a result, solidarity along the lines of the hegemony of class needs to be informed and shaped by solidarity along the lines of gender, sexuality, race, ethnicity, nationality, and so on. Nevertheless, Gramsci's original sense that class in its broadest and most diverse sense—including the so-called subaltern[11]—is part of what guides organic intellectuals is still informative today because neoliberal capitalism never rests and benefits disproportionally from interlocking oppressions on a global scale. This approach is especially relevant for theologians working in the Abrahamic faiths, whose most ancient traditions identify a God who changes the course of history by taking the sides of and standing in solidarity with exploited Hebrew slaves in Egypt (presented in the sacred texts of Judaism, Christianity, and Islam) and the working majorities of Palestine, the Middle East, and ultimately the whole world. Although this is a complex history with many ups and downs, it is a history of alternative powers at work and of transformation.

No doubt, the various ethnic, racial, gendered, sexual, tribal, and national identities of these working majorities

---

11 Gramsci, 52.

were always part of their struggles for liberation, but no struggle can ever be limited to matters of identity alone. The Hebrew slaves, for instance, were both Hebrew and slaves, and gender was part of the struggle as well from the very beginning (recall the Hebrew midwives Shiphrah and Puah, Moses's sister Miriam, Pharaoh's nameless daughter who adopts Moses in the Jewish and Christian traditions, and Pharaoh's wife, Asiya, who in the traditions of Islam saves Moses and accepts his faith). Ultimately, organic intellectuals in the Capitalocene need to ask the question "What are we up against?" and provide answers that take into account the flow of money and capital, which translates not only into economic power but also into political, cultural, and religious power, examining where alternatives are emerging in order to join the struggle there. In the process, identities are shaped and reshaped in touch with divine identities that may be open ended, as already the earliest Abrahamic traditions would find out (Exod 3:14), but stand united in resisting oppression and overcoming exploitation everywhere (Exod 3:15–17).

Nothing less is the task of theology in the Capitalocene if it is to transcend the dominant status quo as well as cheap grace (Dietrich Bonhoeffer) and what we might call cheap sin—theological concepts of sin and destruction that are not substantial enough so that engaging them does not lead to liberation.[12] The organic work of

---

12 In contrast to both insufficient liberal and conservative theological notions of sin, this is the beauty of Anselm of Canterbury's response to Boso's assumption that he could just ask for forgiveness: "You have not yet considered the weight of sin." Anselm of Canterbury, "Cur Deus Homo?," in *Anselm of Canterbury: The Major Works*, ed. Brian Davies

movement and community organizing that is linked to all of this is no longer just the work of activists but one of the most genuine expressions of the faith of religious communities and therefore key to the work of theology in the Capitalocene.[13]

Chapters

The chapters of this book build on one another, but they can also be read out of order. Everyone should read chapter 4, as it addresses the biggest challenge to the dominant system—the deep transnational solidarity of people and the planet that can no longer be pushed aside or misclassified as minorities to be integrated; people and the planet constitute solid majorities everywhere. Chapter 4 is also where those who approach the material of this book with some awareness of pressures along the lines of class, race, gender, and ecology might start to read. Those who are interested in broadening their ecological consciousness should start with chapter 1 and move on to chapter 2. And those who have not given much thought to the realities of class—arguably one of the most underreflected topics at present—might consider starting with chapter 3.

Chapter 1 addresses the life-threatening conditions of climate change—for humans and nonhumans alike—bringing

and G. R. Evans (Oxford: Oxford University Press, 1998), 305. For an interpretation of Anselm's work along these lines, see Joerg Rieger, *Christ & Empire: From Paul to Postcolonial Times* (Minneapolis: Fortress, 2007), chap. 3.

13　This is one of the basic assumptions we are exploring at the Wendland-Cook Program in Religion and Justice at Vanderbilt University Divinity School: http://www.religionandjustice.org.

together the study of ecology, economics, and religion, three disciplines that are rarely put in conversation with one another. Such conversations are at the heart of theology in the Capitalocene. What is threatened by climate change, to be sure, is not the future of life on planet Earth as such but the future of human life as we know it, along with the lives of many other species. Inequalities along the lines of race, ethnicity, sexuality, gender, nationality, and class further exacerbate this scenario. Taking a deeper look at the causes of our current condition, a better grasp of possible solutions develops. Collective human agency that is informed and energized by rising pressures and pending catastrophes has changed the world in the past and may change it again, and neither should the contributions of nonhuman agency be overlooked. Conversations among ecology, economics, and religion show the limits of efforts in each area—religion has often been part of the problem, but so have economic approaches and misdirected ecological efforts—as well as the potential for deep engagements with the challenges posed by the Capitalocene.

Chapter 2 engages concerns that ecological destruction is tied to widespread disdain for material reality, as found in certain religious expressions and time-honored theologies that focus on the transcendent at the expense of the immanent. In response to these concerns, the solution may appear to focus the work of theology on the immanent (the worldly) rather than the transcendent (the otherworldly). However, this focus on the immanent alone may be insufficient, as capitalism fits that bill as well, even though it has been no less damaging to the environment than any focus on the transcendent. The same could be said about the so-called gospel of prosperity. As a result, efforts to resist ecological destruction demand alternative constructive theological solutions that reclaim both the transcendent and the immanent together. In this chapter, the contributions of new materialism in conversation with economic democracy will contribute further to theology in the Capitalocene.

The question of what exploits the planet cannot be answered without exploring what exploits people, and so chapter 3 offers an analysis of class from a theological perspective. In this chapter, widespread misconceptions about class as independent social strata are contrasted with relational understandings of class that offer insights into the flows of power in all areas of life, sometimes dismissed as "class struggle," which turn out to be central to the work of theological reflection. Thinking about class in terms of power opens the door to intersectional awareness of other flows of power, which complexifies the analysis of power and rules out class exclusivism or what has sometimes been called the "oppression Olympics." Moreover, reflections on class and power are not only about critique but also about construction, tied to investigating alternative manifestations of power that are embodied by both humanity and the divine. Postcolonial and subaltern studies, as well as other theoretical and theological developments, further complexify an understanding of class, with consequences for virtually every aspect of theology in the Capitalocene.

Chapter 4 addresses the touchy and seemingly impossible matter of solidarity and ways in which theology in the Capitalocene might reclaim it. Theology, picking up the legacies of the progressive Christian Left—distinct from liberal and other more generic progressive approaches—has much to learn but can also make some valuable contributions in a political and religious climate that is marked by divide-and-conquer as well as unite-and-conquer methods deployed by the profit-driven interests of the Right. "Deep solidarity" turns out to be the opposite of the solidarity of the Right, as it cherishes and creatively deploys diversity rather than uniformity and as it brings together the many to stand up for themselves, while the solidarity of the Right unites the many to stand up for the few. Deep solidarity is intersectional from the outset, as one of its key insights is that privilege does not always translate into power. Moreover, it is built not on pious wishes and moral appeals but on the observation that "if one member suffers, all suffer together with it," as formulated by the apostle Paul (1 Cor 12:26) and reflected in many of the traditions of the progressive Left, religious or not.

The conclusions of the book address one of the most delicate issues in current US politics: reparations for the enslavement of African Americans, linked to confessions of sin, repentance, and conversion enabled by deep solidarity. The topic of reparations continues, extends, and concludes the theological reflections of this book, which are deeply rooted in the material realities of the Capitalocene, as they shape up in the world of productive and reproductive labor of people and the planet. Bringing together race, gender, class, and ecology one more time in ways that go beyond the politics of recognition, the book ends by presenting models of how solidarity builds from the bottom up, with special consideration of the agency and labor of those whose lives are most severely affected and distorted by the intersectional oppressions that mark our time, including final reflections on the agency of the divine, as no one is free until all are free, as civil rights leaders like Fannie Lou Hamer and Dr. Martin Luther King Jr. used to remind us.

1

The Peculiar Agency of People and the Planet

Rethinking Religion and Everything Else

What would most people do if they were diagnosed with a life-threatening condition? They would probably get a second opinion and perhaps a third. Suppose they got one hundred opinions and ninety-seven of them confirmed the existence of a life-threatening condition. Even if, for some reason, they chose to believe the three dissenting opinions, they would probably still take precautionary measures to mitigate harm.

It is now commonly known that 97 percent of scientists agree that human-caused climate change, driven by greenhouse gas emissions like CO_2 and methane, is real.[1] Less well known may be the fact that in the confrontation of climate-change science and climate-change denial, we are

---

1 John Cook et al., "Consensus on Consensus: A Synthesis of Consensus Estimates on Human-Caused Global Warming," *Environmental Research Letters* 11, no. 4 (April 13, 2016), https://iopscience.iop.org/article/10.1088/1748-9326/11/4/048002.

not dealing with two ideas of equal value, not only because of a lack of scientific standards on the minority side of the debate, but also because of firm ideological commitments and disproportionate funding on the side of those who deny climate change.[2]

Becoming aware of climate change amounts to receiving the diagnosis of a life-threatening condition. What is threatened, to be sure, is not the future of life on planet Earth as such but the future of human life as we know it, along with the lives of many other species. Earth, myriads of bacteria, cockroaches, and perhaps even some humans who have the means for survival will likely be fine for the time being; the majority of humanity, hummingbirds, and koalas probably will not. Inequalities along the lines of race, ethnicity, sexuality, gender, nationality, and class further exacerbate this scenario. We will come back to class analysis in chapter 3, as it is currently the most underanalyzed category on this list, and to intersectional analyses of race, gender, and class in chapter 4.

Even if there were only a small chance that human-caused climate change was a problem, these issues would need to be addressed because of the magnitude of the problem, which amounts to matters of life and death for large numbers of people and many ecosystems. Everything is at stake for everyone and everything. As womanist theologian Sofia Betancourt has put it, "We should not allow our fear or

---

2 See the discussion of the problematic role of ideas in the debates around climate change in Laurel Kearns, "Climate Change," in *Grounding Religion: A Field Guide to the Study of Religion and Ecology*, ed. Whitney Bauman, Richard Bohannon, and Kevin J. O'Brien (New York: Routledge, 2017), 141–46.

our rightful sense of immense urgency to legitimize addressing centuries of environmental devastation in isolation from
centuries of human oppression and despair."[3]

Not all is lost just yet. As we take a deeper look at the
causes of our current condition, a better grasp of possible
solutions emerges as well. Social movements and the agency
emerging from those benefiting less from prevailing developments have changed the world in the past and may well
change it again. Neither should the agency of nonhuman
nature be dismissed out of hand, as it is not just a victim but
also an agent and a producer, even if its productions have for
the most part been appropriated as freebies by capitalism.
How would another look at problems and solutions impact
the work of theologians, economists, and social and natural
scientists?

Analytical Tasks

In light of the sheer magnitude of the challenges before us,
it would not be wise to limit ourselves to dealing with symp-
toms only. Yet as we identify the core of these challenges
and search for solutions, much of what we know must be
rethought in one way or another, including dominant cultural assumptions, traditional academic disciplines, and
perhaps most importantly, religion. This chapter, therefore,
seeks to address concerns for the environment as they have
been registered at the grass roots and picked up in theology,

---

3   Sofia Betancourt, "Ethical Implications of Environmental Justice," in *Justice on Earth:
    People of Faith Working at the Intersections of Race, Class, and the Environment*, ed. Manisha
    Mishra-Marzetti and Jennifer Nordstrom (Boston: Skinner House Books, 2018), 44.

sociology, and economics, giving rise to what is now called ecotheology, environmental sociology, and environmental economics.

The role neoliberal capitalism has played in climate change is hard to dispute. At present, 71 percent of CO_2 emissions are linked to only one hundred fossil fuel producers. By comparison, if all Americans eliminated meat from their diet, this would only reduce current US greenhouse gas emissions by 2.6 percent. According to the Intergovernmental Panel on Climate Change, between 1988 and 2016, the fossil fuel industry has emitted as much greenhouse gas as in the previous 237 years since the beginning of the Industrial Revolution.[4]

Since the dawn of capitalism, things have grown exponentially worse, and although new technologies are being developed that limit some CO_2 emissions, capitalism's inherent drive for expansion does not bode well for the future of the climate. Even if the environment were to register more

---

4 See Paul Griffin, "Carbon Majors Report 2017," Carbon Majors Database, CDP, July 2017, https://cdn.cdp.net/cdp-production/cms/reports/documents/000/002/327/original/Carbon-Majors-Report-2017.pdf?1501833772, reporting on the percentage of CO_2 emissions today and since 1988. See also the related fact check: Grace Rahman, "Are 100 Companies Causing 71% of Carbon Emissions?," Full Fact, November 1, 2018, https://fullfact.org/news/are-100-companies-causing-71-carbon-emissions/. Brett Clark and Richard York, "Carbon Metabolism: Global Capitalism, Climate Change, and the Biospheric Rift," *Theory and Society* 34, no. 4 (August 2005): 403 (referencing a 1995 Intergovernmental Panel on Climate Change report); also note that, according to the Intergovernmental Panel on Climate Change, the amount of CO_2 in the atmosphere has risen by 31 percent since the onset of industrialization, and half of that increase happened between 1965 and 1995. Regarding meat consumption, see Frank M. Mitloehner, "Yes, Eating Meat Affects the Environment, but Cows Are Not Killing the Climate," Conversation, April 29, 2021, https://theconversation.com/yes-eating-meat-affects-the-environment-but-cows-are-not-killing-the-climate-94968.

in economic calculations (currently, the environment is still mostly considered an "externality" in capitalist economics), this would not be sufficient. In order to maximize profits for shareholders—the declared goal of capitalist economies, backed by legal precedents—environmental costs are pushed as low as possible, paralleling the push on the costs of labor.

Nature and labor are among the "seven cheap things" on which the history of the present-day world rests, along with cheap money, care, food, energy, and lives.[5] The labor of enslaved people—both past and present—and the reproductive labor of women (including gestational labor) provide the most severe examples of these dynamics, as these forms of labor have often been more closely identified with nonhuman nature than with productive labor and therefore have mostly been unpaid and treated as externalities![6] In the process, capitalism has transformed the globe: no part of the so-called natural environment is left unaffected, and hardly any place in the world is left untouched. In the United States, only about 7 percent of old-growth forest is left, defined as areas that have not been used by humans in at least a century, and since 1600, about 90 percent of the virgin forests that covered much of the United States have been cleared

---

5   These seven cheap things are discussed in Raj Patel and Jason W. Moore, *A History of the World in Seven Cheap Things: A Guide to Capitalism, Nature, and the Future of the Planet* (Oakland: University of California Press, 2017).

6   Jason W. Moore, "The Rise of Cheap Nature," in Moore, *Anthropocene or Capitalocene?*, 79: "Backed by imperial power and capitalist rationality, it mobilized the unpaid work and energy of humans—especially women, especially the enslaved—in the service of transforming landscapes with a singular purpose: the endless accumulation of capital."

away.[7] The tropics, to give another example, now feature crops like sugar, tobacco, and coffee, which took over much of the natural vegetation with the help of the tools of the natural sciences.[8] The result is not just the transformation of nonhuman nature but also the transformation of traditional ways of life and human labor, productive and reproductive.

Here lies a key to our analytical task because this economic logic is more foundational than it may appear at first sight, affecting virtually everything else. It is not merely a matter of accounting and bookkeeping, as it lies at the heart of the histories of colonialism and neocolonialism, religion and theology, culture, and politics as well as of the histories of slavery and labor under the conditions of capitalism from the very beginning. This is also where the constructs of race, ethnicity, gender, and sexuality find some of their most damaging expressions. Phenomena like environmental racism, when seen from this perspective, are not just about the dumping of toxic waste in racial minority neighborhoods; they are about shaping people to the core, keeping in check their agency, the fruits of their labor, and any attempts to live in constructive relationships with the agency of nonhuman nature. This is why efforts at preservation and conservation are never sufficient and can often become complicit with oppression and exploitation. Preservationist John Muir's celebrated efforts, for instance, not only overlooked

---

7 Brant Ran, "How Much Old Growth Forest Remains in the US?—the Understory," Rainforest Action Network, November 11, 2008, https://www.ran.org/the-understory/how_much_old_growth_forest_remains_in_the_us/.

8 Justin McBrien, "Accumulating Extinction: Planetary Catastrophism in the Necrocene," in Moore, *Anthropocene or Capitalocene?*, 120–21.

the existence of native populations; they also ignored the advances of capitalism that made the preservation of certain areas desirable in the first place.[9]

Another factor leading to climate change and to ecological destruction more generally has, arguably, been religion, and Christianity in particular. As historian Lynn White argued in a now classic 1967 article in *Science*, Western Christianity in its Latin forms has significantly contributed to the problem of ecological destruction. According to White, Western Christianity is "the most anthropocentric religion the world has seen,"[10] playing off humanity and the nonhuman natural world and leading to the devaluation and destruction of the latter on a grand scale. The problem, according to White, is not just with religion but also with other expressions of Western culture, including modern science, because even post-Christian Western culture continues to be shaped by this overemphasis on humanity and its related disregard for nonhuman nature. Much more could be said about this, as White is just scratching the surface. For our purposes, we might add the social sciences to this mix, whose very name indicates an emphasis on the human over the nonhuman, linked to the classical division of academic disciplines that is only gradually overcome today in areas like environmental sociology and postcolonial approaches to science and theology.

In the past five decades since White's clarion call, there have been various responses. In the natural sciences, the

---

9   McBrien, 124.
10 Lynn White, "The Historical Roots of Our Ecologic Crisis," *Science* 155, no. 3767 (March 10, 1967): 1205.

study of human-caused climate change is one example of how an anthropocentric view of the world may be challenged. In the social sciences, the emergence of environmental sociology is an example not just of the expansion of a discipline but of substantial changes in the conception of what counts as social relations, taking into account that society shapes nonhuman nature and that nonhuman nature shapes society.[11] In the study of religion and theology, some theologians have picked up White's critique and attempted to reclaim alternative theological traditions that are less anthropocentric. After all, White challenged not only anthropocentrism but also the inability to conceive of positive relationships between the divine and nonhuman nature. In response, it was pointed out that such relationships are more common in the history of Christianity than White realized—the work of many theologians influenced by the thought of the Romantic period and transcendentalism may serve as an example—and today many of these relationships are widely reclaimed in ecotheological circles. One of the most prominent examples is the late Vanderbilt theologian Sallie McFague's notion of the world as God's body.[12]

Referencing the role of religion, another look at the bigger picture is called for. Scholars of religion and theology, although they might feel flattered that their subject matter is considered so important, also need to broaden their horizons. White's broad critique of modernity exemplifies

---

11 Clark and York, "Carbon Metabolism," 398. Already Karl Marx, engaging the work of soil chemists like Justus von Liebig, talked about the "metabolic interaction" between humans and the earth (398).

12 Sallie McFague, *The Body of God: An Ecological Theology* (Minneapolis: Fortress, 1993).

the problem, as he missed important developments of the bigger picture—in particular, the metamorphoses of capitalism. This topic often drops out also in the study of theology, religion, and even some of the natural and social sciences.[13] The common descriptor of the current age as the *Anthropocene*—found across various academic disciplines—signals the problem. A closer look at the relevance of capitalism to our topic suggests a change of terminologies: more appropriate than the term *Anthropocene* would be the term *Capitalocene*, given that in the current situation, capital, power, and nature are closely related.[14] In other words, blaming humanity as a whole for climate change and ecological destruction misses the flows of power that determine our age. The same would be true for blaming religion as such or all sciences, natural or social.

A key question is thus how various fields of study (natural and social sciences, economics, the study of theology and religion) are tied to the realities of capitalism that shape our age, for good and for ill, and what deeper encounters between these fields might accomplish as we address climate change and ecological destruction more broadly. The framing will come not from a neutral place, as there are no such places, but from solidarity with those most adversely affected. As Indian theologian George Zachariah puts it, "The subaltern oppositional gaze does not begin with grand

---

13 For White, there does not even seem to be a qualitative difference between the economics of the early Middle Ages and later capitalist developments.

14 For the term *Capitalocene*, see Moore, "Anthropocene or Capitalocene?," 1–12. Moore, "Rise of Cheap Nature," 81, notes the organic relation of capital, power, and nature, and later he talks about capitalism as a new way of organizing the relations among nature, work, reproduction, and "the conditions of life" (85).

ecological and cosmological visions and narrative; rather, it begins with issues of survival and livelihood."[15] A feminist Indian theologian, Aruna Gnanadason, reminds us that issues of livelihood and survival are at the core of Indian women's concerns for ecology and economics, as the majority of them are poor.[16] There is a distinct difference between what has been called the "environmentalism of the rich" and the "environmentalism of the poor," which needs to be explored further.[17]

Classical Positions in Environmental Economics, Ecological Social Science, and Ecological Theology

While religious and theological studies often tend to employ the history of ideas even when engaging environmental and economic concerns, a closer look at social-scientific and economic paradigms will be instructive. In theological studies in particular, the broader horizon of the social sciences and economics was introduced by various liberation theologies in the 1970s, but much is still to be learned, especially in conversation with ecological and environmental studies. In the social sciences, ecological social science work has been pursued since the 1960s.[18] Two theoretical paradigms

---

15 George Zachariah, *Alternatives Unincorporated: Earth Ethics from the Grassroots*, Cross Cultural Theologies (London: Equinox, 2011), 102.

16 David G. Hallman and Aruna Gnanadason, "Women, Economy and Ecology," in *Eco-theology: Voices from the South and North* (Maryknoll, NY: Orbis Books, 1994), 180.

17 Hannah Holleman, *Dust Bowls of Empire: Imperialism, Environmental Politics, and the Injustice of "Green" Capitalism*, Yale Agrarian Studies (New Haven, CT: Yale University Press, 2018), 159.

18 I would like to thank PhD student in environmental sociology Annika Rieger, Boston College, for her contributions to the following descriptions of ecological modernization

relevant to our discussion arose in the 1980s: the "treadmill of production" (ToP)[19] and "ecological modernization" (EM).[20]

In both paradigms, the economy is the central concern. Similar to efforts that seek to bring together ecology and religion, environmental social scientists have sought to bring together ecology and economy based on the insight that an economy that neglects ecology becomes destructive of it, just like a religion that neglects ecology. Both positions share an understanding that the basic cause of ecological destruction and climate change is not anthropocentrism, as White argued, but the economic system of capitalism that organizes human action. In the so-called Capitalocene, not all of humanity, and not even the majority of humanity, is driving the exploitation of the nonhuman environment and benefiting from it—just like the majority of humanity is hardly benefiting from the exploitation of human labor or from the largely uncontrolled CO_2 emissions produced by neoliberal capitalism.

Despite agreement on the importance of the economy, however, EM and ToP are often found in conflict with each

---

and the treadmill of production. For our coauthored work on the topic, see Joerg Rieger and Annika Rieger, "Working with Environmental Economists," in *T&T Clark Handbook of Christian Theology and Climate Change*, ed. E. M. Conradie and Hilda P. Koster (London: Bloomsbury T&T Clark, 2020), 53–64.

19 Allan Schnaiberg, *The Environment: From Surplus to Scarcity* (New York: Oxford University Press, 1980).

20 Udo Ernst Simonis, "Ecological Modernization of Industrial Society: Three Strategic Elements," in *Economy and Ecology: Towards Sustainable Development*, ed. Franco Archibugi and Peter Nijkam (Dordrecht: Springer, 1989), 119–37; Gert Spaargaren and Arthur P.J. Mol, "Sociology, Environment, and Modernity: Ecological Modernization as a Theory of Social Change," *Society & Natural Resources* 5, no. 4 (1992): 323–44.

other. After all, EM sees the current economic system as salvageable when modified, while ToP sees the current economic system as the source of the problem so that the only solution is its overthrow and replacement with a new system. Similar disagreements about the role of economics can be found in theological approaches dealing with the environment, as we shall see.

EM theory argues that capitalism can become more "green" and that societies can become more sustainable and reduce their environmental impact by utilizing the progress of technology, supported by pressure from interest groups that push corporations and dominant institutions to prioritize the environment. EM theorists argue that rather than thinking of the environment as external to economic concerns, it can be brought into economic equations and adequately accounted for, and this process will force corporations to face the true costs of business and encourage them to invest in "greening" their production.[21] In this model, the political process is of special importance because the government is seen as the institution that is most likely to be able to implement pressure and encourage changes toward sustainability.[22] Sustainability is important to the theory in two senses—EM asks how economic institutions can become environmentally sustainable in order for the institutions themselves to be sustainable and continue their existence.

---

21 Spaargaren and Mol, "Sociology, Environment, and Modernity," 334–36.

22 Frederick H. Buttel, "Ecological Modernization as Social Theory," *Geoforum* 31, no. 1 (2000): 57–65. Suggestions for policy are important to most EM studies, either to help mitigate current damage or to prevent future degradation. Spaargaren and Mol, "Sociology, Environment, and Modernity," 338–41.

The approaches of Christian mainline denominations often resemble this approach, as they share concerns for greening institutions while maintaining their existence and conventional ideas of God. This can be seen, for instance, not only in efforts to save energy and to install solar panels on the roofs of church buildings; it can also be seen in more courageous efforts to divest ecclesial endowments from funds linked to carbon emissions without challenging the capitalist logic of growth. Examples include investor efforts like Climate Action 100+ that successfully put pressure on the world's largest greenhouse gas emitters to reduce emissions.[23] These efforts are admirable, but institutional stability and growth continue to be central values. The dynamics of EM also find parallels in theological approaches that support the principles of capitalism while trying to make it greener and perhaps somewhat more just. Images of God commonly found at work in these approaches tend to envision God in terms of the dominant institutions, as the sustainer and reformer of the status quo.[24]

ToP theory, on the other hand, targets an institutional system that prioritizes profits and economic growth, aimed at increasing productivity, which results in environmentally detrimental outcomes.[25] At the root of ecological destruction is the economic system of capitalism, requiring increasing levels of production and consumption of material goods to

---

23 See the website of Climate Action 100+, http://www.climateaction100.org.

24 See, for instance, Brent Waters, *Just Capitalism: A Christian Ethic of Economic Globalization* (Louisville, KY: Westminster John Knox, 2016).

25 Allan Schnaiberg, "Sustainable Development and the Treadmill of Production," in *The Politics of Sustainable Development: Theory, Policy and Practice within the European Union*, ed. Susan Baker et al. (London: Routledge, 1997), 75.

maintain economic growth and ensure its existence.[26] Economic progress is likely to increase resource extraction, hazardous waste, pollution, and other forms of ecological destruction, eventually culminating in climate change. Sociologists like Richard York, John Bellamy Foster, and others have weighed in, arguing that a new economic order is necessary to end the cycle of environmental harm. EM's hope of lowering the environmental impact over time based on technological innovation, by contrast, is due to an increased variability across phenomena (like increased gas mileage of some cars) but overlooks that the overall situation continues to worsen (like the overall gas consumption in the United States because cars are getting heavier).[27] The same would be true for the adoption of self-driving electric vehicles if savings result in more frequent or longer trips and if better traffic flow results in increased traffic. ToP, therefore, presents an encompassing critique of the economic status quo of capitalism since its beginnings, which makes solutions more difficult to identify. At the same time, it also opens up the possibility of cooperation with other social justice movements that present similar critiques and work toward shared goals.

While this approach finds fewer parallels in Christian communities, it encounters kindred spirits in the work of some ecologically minded theologians and scholars of

---

26 Allan Schnaiberg, David N. Pellow, and Adam Weinberg, "The Treadmill of Production and the Environmental State," in *The Environmental State under Pressure*, ed. Arthur P. J. Mol and Fredrick H. Buttel, vol. 10 (New York: JAI Press, 2002), 15–32.

27 Richard York, "The Treadmill of (Diversifying) Production," *Organization & Environment* 17, no. 3 (September 2004): 360.

religion who have engaged in matters of economics for some time.[28] Some of these approaches tend to envision images of God as presenting fundamental challenges to the logic of the capitalist economic status quo, linking them to emerging alternatives instead. Theologian John Cobb and economist Herman Daly, for instance, have promoted a "steady-state economy," which does not require the constant growth that is a fundamental demand of capitalism. Unlike ToP, however, Cobb and Daly are not rejecting capitalism altogether, as they merely envision a capitalism with less growth.[29] Other theological approaches are more critical of capitalism (see below), but efforts to put together alternative economic and ecological thought are still in their beginnings in the field of theological studies.[30]

Since their inception, ToP and EM theories have clashed in various ways. The originator of ToP, Allan Schnaiberg, is critical of EM's faith in the capitalist system he sees as the source of environmental destruction. He also challenges EM's main solution, the idea that technological innovation is the key to environmental sustainability, arguing that no matter how much technology improves, it will never be

---

28 See, for instance, from a Christian perspective, Herman E. Daly and John B. Cobb, *For the Common Good: Redirecting the Economy toward Community, the Environment, and a Sustainable Future*, 2nd ed. (Boston: Beacon, 1994); and from a Buddhist perspective, Ernst F. Schumacher, *Small Is Beautiful: Economics as If People Mattered* (New York: Harper & Row, 1973).

29 Daly and Cobb, *For the Common Good*.

30 For some initial efforts, see the contributions of the Wendland-Cook Program in Religion and Justice at Vanderbilt, including a webinar series on Liberating People and the Planet (https://www.religionandjustice.org/liberating) and a blog series on Climate Change and Capitalism (https://www.religionandjustice.org/interventions-forum-climate-change-and-capitalism).

enough to balance out capitalism's need for the increase of production and consumption.[31] Another common critique of EM is that it cherry-picks case studies,[32] usually selecting industries from northern Europe that have implemented diverse technologies and instigated their own efforts at environmental protection. EM theorists acknowledge this focus, but they do not see it as a failing of their theory. They argue that the Netherlands and Germany, the countries from which most EM case studies are drawn, are simply the countries that are currently best implementing the ideals of EM and that they show potential ways in which capitalist industrialization can be environmentally beneficial.[33] ToP theorists respond that the case studies of EM theorists show no proof that modernization *as a whole* is encouraging sustainability at any level.[34]

The defense that EM theorists give for their theory is that ToP is more concerned with "academic debates" about "philosophy" than the actual "questions raised by activists and policy makers."[35] They see ToP as having limited value because of what they consider to be idealist and utopian tendencies that do not produce real-world solutions.[36] EM theorists argue that their theory can provide practical and applicable solutions to environmental problems that utilize

---

31 Schnaiberg, "Sustainable Development," 76–77.

32 Richard York and Eugene A. Rosa, "Key Challenges to Ecological Modernization Theory," *Organization & Environment* 16, no. 3 (September 1, 2003): 280–81.

33 Spaargaren and Mol, "Sociology, Environment, and Modernity," 324; Buttel, "Ecological Modernization," 39.

34 York and Rosa, "Key Challenges," 382.

35 Arthur P. J. Mol and Gert Spaargaren, "Ecological Modernisation Theory in Debate: A Review," *Environmental Politics* 9, no. 1 (2000): 39.

36 Buttel, "Ecological Modernization," 60–61.

existing tools such as development, modernization, and innovation.[37] Focusing on reform rather than replacement, EM theorists believe that working within the economic system can solve the current environmental crisis.

Similar tensions between fundamental critiques of capitalism and efforts to ameliorate it can also be found in theological debates, even though the focus is typically more on intellectual disagreements than actual empirical studies. Like ToP, systemic critiques like those of various liberation theologies have also often been accused of being idealistic and utopian. Such charges are often quickly leveled against those who are questioning the foundations of the dominant systems, but they overlook the actual struggles on the ground to which each of these approaches is linked and the progress that has been made in building grassroots power. At the same time, it cannot be denied that some of the more reformist theologies of the mainline that are closer to the centers of the Capitalocene have had a certain success as well, like promoting efforts to recycle or to save energy and perhaps even to divest from fossil fuel. Nevertheless, these successes have provided little evidence of their ability to transform systemic problems and turn things around at levels that would make a sustained difference in the ongoing struggle against greenhouse gas emissions and climate change.

In sum, the urgency of climate change threatening human survival does not allow anyone to claim victory in the debates at this time, pushing instead for a closer look at the problems and more creative reflections. But while each of the positions

---

37 Mol and Spaargaren, "Ecological Modernisation Theory," 334–38.

discussed has contributions to make, seeking the solution of a middle road would be insufficient, according to the advice of seventeenth-century German poet Friedrich von Logau: "In situations of danger and great need, the middle road leads to death."[38]

Production versus Consumption

The divergence between ToP and EM has to do with diametrically opposed assessments of the role of capitalism as solution or problem. This is linked to differences in what is identified as the source of ecological destruction and climate change and whether more damage to the environment comes from the consumption or the production of material goods (we will get to reproduction shortly).

When theologians have engaged economic underpinnings of ecological destruction, consumption has often been the primary target. McFague, one of the earliest ecotheologians, has focused on consumerism, correcting her prior assumption that the problem of ecological destruction is not a lack of love of nature but the temptation of overconsumption. Many other theologians have put forth similar arguments, and this logic is also widespread in many mainline Christian communities.[39]

---

38 "In Gefahr und grosser Not bringt der Mittel-Weg den Tod" (English translation mine). Friedrich von Logau, *Sämmtliche Sinngedichte*, ed. Gustav Eitner (Tübingen, Germany: Litterarischer Verein, 1872), 421.

39 Sallie McFague, *Life Abundant: Rethinking Theology and Economy for a Planet in Peril* (Minneapolis: Fortress, 2001), xi, 33. The works of ethicists Cynthia Moe-Lobeda and William T. Cavanaugh emphasize consumption in different ways as well.

In my own work, by contrast, I have argued that theological challenges to capitalism need to pay more attention to production because problems of consumption are directly tied to the capitalist need for growing economic production, typically mediated to consumers by the advertising industry (reproduction and reproductive labor are the condition of production but often not even mentioned because they are relegated to minoritized human and nonhuman labor).[40] If consumption is seen as linked to the capitalist need to constantly increase production, a more profound analysis and critique of capitalism replaces common moral condemnations of consumerism. Blaming consumers for consumerism not only fails to address what drives the production of consumers' desires; it also covers up the causes.

The disagreement as to from which side of the production/consumption dynamic ecological destruction originates results in solutions targeting different sides of the dynamic. While even EM theory recognizes that production has created ecological problems, it sees the further development of industry as the only path toward solving those problems.[41] This understanding of the problem encourages solutions that focus on consumption: that is, introducing new technologies, changing consumer patterns to be more ecologically minded, and introducing environmental and sustainability values. EM sees innovation—in the form of new regulations, industrial processes, technologies, and consumer demands—as our best hope for dealing with ecological degradation and

---

40 Joerg Rieger, *No Rising Tide: Theology, Economics, and the Future* (Minneapolis: Fortress, 2009), chap. 4.

41 York and Rosa, "Key Challenges," 274.

capitalism as the economic system best suited to encourage these innovations.

One of the solutions often proffered by EM theorists is implementing technology in as many realms as possible. Information and communication technologies, for instance, might have the potential to decouple consumption and material goods. This decoupling would allow for growth with limited environmental effects because consumption levels would require fewer material resources, which would solve the "sustainability dilemma": the paradox that arises when the adoption of the consumption levels of "developed" countries by "developing" countries presents an irreconcilable ecological burden.[42] If consumption were decoupled from material goods, "developing" countries could adopt the consumption levels of "developed" countries without burdening the environment. Even without the possibility of dematerialization, the implementation of technology to increase the efficiency of production would enable more goods to be produced with fewer resources and less waste.

ToP theorists, on the other hand, see the suggestions offered by EM theorists as short-term solutions rooted in a focus on the wrong "end" of the economic equation. ToP theorists focus on the production side rather than the consumption side of the dynamic because they argue, as I have in my own work, that production is driven not by consumer

---

42   Lorenz M. Hilty and Thomas F. Ruddy, "Sustainable Development and ICT Interpreted in a Natural Science Context," *Information, Communication & Society* 13, no. 1 (February 2010): 8–12, https://doi.org/10.1080/13691180903322805.

demand but rather by the demands of capitalism.[43] If this is correct, the only way to stop environmentally harmful practices is to target the root of the problem: the capitalist production system. While to their critics, the call for sweeping economic reforms seems unrealistic, ToP theorists see global social movements such as the Landless Worker's Movement (Movimento dos Trabalhadores Sem Terra [MST] in Brazil), the World Social Forum, and others as offering solutions. Many of these social movements call for broad social change, including economic change, and they have been able to mobilize people not only to demand change but to enact it. While these groups coalesce around different social problems, they are able to wield bottom-up, democratic power by organizing larger groups of people and thereby challenging the basis of the global capitalist ToP system that produces climate change.

In the study of theology, more profound critiques of capitalism and support for social movements have been developed by diverse liberation theologies for over half a century. While liberation theologies have often been considered to be primarily concerned with human oppression and exploitation, matters of ecology have long been part of the conversation. The work of Brazilian liberation theologians Leonardo Boff and Ivone Gebara may serve as examples.[44] The ecofeminist work of Gebara, in particular, is deeply connected to poor

---

43 Schnaiberg, Pellow, and Gould, "Treadmill of Production," 19–24; Rieger, *No Rising Tide*, chap. 4.

44 Leonardo Boff, *Cry of the Earth, Cry of the Poor*, trans. Philip Berryman (Maryknoll, NY: Orbis Books, 1997); Ivone Gebara, *Longing for Running Water: Ecofeminism and Liberation* (Minneapolis: Fortress, 1999).

people's movements, especially the everyday experiences of women in impoverished Brazilian neighborhoods, where she resides.[45] In my own work, I have addressed the importance of movements like the Occupy Wall Street movement and the accomplishments of the international labor movement, which have not only changed economic relationships but also contributed to the fight against racism and sexism in places where it hurts people the most.[46] In these theologies, images of God develop in the midst of the struggle, with the divine inhabiting not only the world in general (as most ecological theologians would agree) but specific contexts of pressure, in solidarity with struggling humanity, the earth, and movements for liberation.

In all of this, the emphasis on production is crucial, as it not only identifies the core of the problem but also can help reclaim agency. Going forward, attention to the dynamics of production still needs to be investigated in terms of the parallels between human and nonhuman agency, including a clearer sense of the place of reproduction that seems to be underdeveloped in ToP. We now understand that where the goal of production is the generation of profits—the categorical imperative of the Capitalocene—production must drive consumption, evolving in a vicious cycle that results

---

45 Gebara, *Longing for Running Water*, 103–4, identifies God in terms of "relatedness as a continual presence that is made explicitly in different ways in different beings," uniting immanence and transcendence (a reference to Sallie McFague). For an engagement of Boff, Gebara, and McFague, see Joerg Rieger, "Reenvisioning Ecotheology and the Divine from the Margins," *Ecotheology* 9, no. 1 (April 2004): 65–85.

46 Joerg Rieger and Kwok Pui-lan, *Occupy Religion: Theology of the Multitude* (Harrisburg, PA: Rowman & Littlefield, 2012); Joerg Rieger and Rosemarie Henkel-Rieger, *Unified We Are a Force: How Faith and Labor Can Overcome America's Inequalities* (St. Louis: Chalice, 2016).

in ecological destruction and climate change. ToP would remind us that exploitation of nonhuman nature is part of the capitalist drive of production, but this dynamic is also manifest in the exploitation of human labor, productive and reproductive. These connections need to be explored further, not least since the labor of enslaved people and the reproductive labor of women are often exploited in similar ways to nonhuman nature.

Of course, analysis and critique alone are insufficient and are easily charged with idealism. Pushing the conversation to the next level are efforts to reclaim specific forms of production as not only the location of the problem but also the place from which alternatives are emerging. For good reasons, one of the most enduring social movements of modern times has been the labor movement. Even though this movement has its own shortcomings and faces numerous challenges today—many of them having to do with pushback because of its success—it still has the potential to address some of the problems of production and transform them. The power of productive (and reproductive) labor as a revolutionary force also manifests itself today in an emerging worker cooperative movement that is global and highly diverse, with historical roots in minority communities, as we will see below.

Keep in mind that capitalist production is never purely about capital itself but about a fundamental production and reproduction of relationships among wealth, power, and nonhuman nature (more about that in chapter 3). If production and reproduction is where relationships are formed, it is also where they need to be reformed, including matters of culture, religion, and theology. Isolating religion and theology from this nexus raises serious questions. Can anything be isolated in an increasingly interconnected world? Why are religion and theology so often failing to recognize how they are shaped by relations of power? And what difference could religion and theology—perceived as independent—be expected to make in an interconnected world determined by various flows of power? Here, scholars of religion and theology need to rethink their fields of study.

Reconsidering and Reclaiming Production, Reproduction, and Agency

If the topics of production and reproduction, and therefore of the agency of the working majority and of the planet, are developed further, new possibilities emerge for transformation. As Jason Moore has argued, "If indeed capitalism is defined by its commitment to endless accumulation, then our starting point—and point of return—must be work."[47] To be sure, work includes all forms of work, formal and informal, and not least the reproductive and mostly unpaid labor of nonhuman nature and of women in patriarchal society. The ability to determine, shape, and reshape work and relationships of work holds the key to a profound transformation of the current situation of ecological destruction that goes hand in hand with the exploitation of people and the planet. Moore puts it with unmistakable clarity: "Shut down a coal plant, and you slow global warming for a day;

---

[47] Moore, "Rise of Cheap Nature," 93.

shut down the relations that made the coal plant, and you can stop it for good."[48]

In the meantime, new ways forward that combine some of the traits of ToP and EM have been proposed in the work of sociologist Juliet Schor and others in the fields of environmental sociology and economics. While Schor challenges consumerism (like EM), she is also attuned to the underlying economic challenges that come from capitalist business as usual (like ToP). Schor and some of her collaborators suggest a new economic model that takes its cues from both emerging grassroots movements and ecological models. Here, ecological thinking is not subordinated to economic thinking but developed in conversation with it. These approaches resonate with the work of theologians like Cobb and others who have added theological reflection to the conversations of economics and ecology. Cobb, for instance, suggests images of God not as a powerful and transcendent overlord or the representative of economic elites but as an entity caring for all creatures, suffering and rejoicing with them, and appreciating diversity.[49] Putting ecological, economic, and theological reflections in conversation is necessary because the problems leading to climate change are linked to all of these fields, which mutually reinforce one another.

Already fathers of neoliberal capitalism, like Friedrich von Hayek, built their theories on certain ecological models, combining ecological, economic, and even theological

---

48　Moore, 94.

49　John B. Cobb, "Christianity, Economics, and Ecology," in *Christianity and Ecology: Seeking the Well-Being of Earth and Humans*, ed. Dieter T. Hessel and Rosemary Radford Ruether (Cambridge: Center for the Study of World Religions, 2000), 508.

elements. A specific interpretation of biological evolution provides the basis for the neoliberal economic emphasis on competition as natural and necessary for flourishing. The often-referenced evolutionary principle of "survival of the fittest," for instance, is taken to mean competition of all against all. In addition, Hayek's economic thought displays theological affinities. As Brazilian theologian Jung Mo Sung has pointed out, the logic of Hayek's position demands a deity that requires sacrifices from some for the flourishing of others, which Sung interprets to the contrary to the logic of Christianity.[50] Challenging Hayek's ecological arguments, Juliet Schor and Craig Thompson have taken on Hayek's social Darwinism, pointing out that more recent understandings of biological evolution challenge ideas of competition and develop a sense of cooperation and symbiotic relationships instead.[51] Such cooperation does not diminish values like agency and diversity but supports them, as it is built on various specializations and adaptations to harsh environments.

While these alternative ecological models still seem to bear some resemblances to neoliberal economic themes—decentralized rather than centralized approaches and appreciation for markets rather than planned economies—they defy neoliberal economics by redefining success and

---

50 See the critiques of Jung Mo Sung, *Desire, Market, and Religion: Horizons of Hope in Complex Societies* (New York: Palgrave Macmillan, 2011), 78–84.

51 Juliet B. Schor and Craig J. Thompson, "Cooperative Networks, Participatory Markets, and Rhizomatic Resistance: Situating Plenitude within Contemporary Political Economy Debates," in *Sustainable Lifestyles and the Quest for Plenitude: Case Studies of the New Economy*, ed. Juliet B. Schor and Craig J. Thompson (New Haven, CT: Yale University Press, 2014), 240–41.

emphasizing interconnectedness rather than the illusion of individualism (discussed in the introduction). In fact, core elements of neoliberal economics are picked up and turned around: markets in the new paradigm, for instance, are defined not by competition where winner takes all but by forms of cooperative networks that might be described as "rhizomatic." The trope of the rhizome, suggested by Schor and Thompson, signifies complex biological root systems that spread and thrive underground and that are hard to uproot.[52] The decentralized nature of such rhizomes stands in stark contrast to neoliberal decentralization. Extending the conversation beyond Schor and Thompson's argument, I would argue that what is overcome here is not neoliberalism's supposed individualism (which is but the myth of the powerful who use it to cover up their connectedness) but neoliberalism's own rhizomatic forms that connect the wealthy and powerful in ways that are highly effective but cleverly kept out of sight.

Developing the themes of rhizomes and connectedness, some scholars of religion and theology have gone even further, arguing that humans need to understand themselves as inextricable parts of the ecology. In the words of Whitney Bauman, humans need to think of themselves as "becoming plant, animal, mineral"[53] because human bodies include all these realities at all times, whether they are aware of it or not. In such a model, the divine finds its place within ecology as well, as involved in the world rather than separate from it.

---

52   Schor and Thompson, 245, with reference to Gilles Deleuze and Félix Guattari.
53   Whitney A. Bauman, *Religion and Ecology: Developing a Planetary Ethic* (New York: Columbia University Press, 2014), 155, also referencing Deleuze and Guattari.

The technical term, commonly used in theological circles, is panentheism, which signals the presence of the divine in everything without identifying God with everything.[54]

In these ecological models, alternative forms of productivity and agency are found not primarily in individuals (whether human, nonhuman, or divine) but in organized cooperatives that are interconnected at the (grass) roots rather than at the level of the elites. Here, a very different kind of economy develops. In neoliberal economies, productivity and agency are supposed to be individual, to be exchanged on the market where all individuals supposedly have equal opportunity, covering up the fact that some are exponentially more powerful and privileged than others and that some never even got a chance (consider the difference between those who run multinational corporations and others for whom opportunities to provide for themselves and their families are simply out of reach). The heart of ecological economics, by contrast, is tied to collective forms of production, reproduction, and agency that mitigate power differentials because they shape up in worker and consumer cooperatives, community-supported agriculture, communal networks, and alternative communities that are often most vital in minority communities and led by women.[55] Added

---

54   This is how the difference between panentheism and pantheism is often explained, although pantheism may not have to be understood literally, either, as identifying God with everything.

55   See the case studies in Schor and Thompson, *Sustainable Lifestyles*; see also Kelsey Ryan-Simkins and Elaine Nogueira-Godsey, "Tangible Actions toward Solidarity: An Ecofeminist Analysis of Women's Participation in Food Justice," in *Valuing Lives, Healing Earth: Religion, Gender, and Life on Earth*, ed. Lilian Dube et al., vol. 3 (Leuven, Belgium: Peeters, 2021), 203–22.

to that list should be various labor movements, both formal and informal, that also aim at alternative productivity and agency (not merely wages and benefits) and thus can also contribute to limiting the most destructive consequences of neoliberal capitalism for people and the planet.

These alternative kinds of production, reproduction, and agency tend to go easier on the planet because ecological destruction directly affects communities where they work and live. Moreover, these kinds of production, reproduction, and agency have the potential to counteract ecological destruction because their primary goal is not infinite growth and the maximization of profits at all costs but more egalitarian relationships and "a commitment to live within the limits of the biosphere."[56] This dynamic does not need to be based on ethereal moral values or abstract religious ideas; its roots are found in the communal self-interest of people who live in specific ecological webs of life whose flourishing—both human and nonhuman—is the foundation for the flourishing of all.

In parallel, theologians also have argued for broadened notions of production, reproduction, and agency that resist the modern capitalist myth of the individual as the supposedly supreme economic agent. Bauman, for instance, talks about agency in relation to our "biohistories." In a different vein, the collective agency of working people and the planet has also been emphasized by a few theologians, and it is at the heart of the Wendland-Cook Program in Religion

---

56 Juliet B. Schor and Craig J. Thompson, "Introduction: Practicing Plenitude," in Schor and Thompson, *Sustainable Lifestyles*, 7.

and Justice at Vanderbilt University Divinity School.[57] In the future, emerging human and nonhuman agency will need to be explored in much more detail, picking up on Karl Marx's classic sense (developed in the seventeenth century by economist William Petty), expressed in somewhat outdated language, that labor is the "father" and nature the "mother" of wealth. The productive and reproductive labor of people and the planet may well be at the roots of revolutionary agency in our time.

Revolutionary Agency

Ecological economics resists extreme inequalities through shared productivity and shared ownership of economic and ecological means of production and reproduction. At the core is a new productive and reproductive base of the economy, composed of new kinds of agency emerging in small-scale green enterprises, cooperative businesses, and popular access to capital. This brings together three concerns: the production and reproduction of wealth, the restoration of ecosystems, and local empowerment. In this model, production and reproduction change hands from being organized by dominant capitalist interests to being organized by communal interests, a shift that is significant in various ways: most importantly, power is relocated into the hands of those

---

57 Bauman, *Religion and Ecology*, 165. For the agency of working people, see Rieger and Henkel-Rieger, *Unified*. This theme is rarely developed by other theologians, but see the short passage in Daly and Cobb, *For the Common Good*, 298–314. See also the website of the Wendland-Cook Program in Religion and Justice, http://www.religionandjustice .org.

who are actually doing the work (in conjunction with non-human nature) and whose interest is tied to their local communities and the natural environment where they live. This relocation of power has fundamental implications for the correction of the dramatic maldistribution of wealth and of inequalities along the lines of race, ethnicity, gender, and sexuality (see chapter 4).

This is the place of worker organizing and of worker cooperatives in line with what economist Richard Wolff has called worker self-directed enterprises.[58] Such economic models, based on cooperation among working people, are more than mere reforms of capitalism, as the basic concern is no longer the unlimited increase of profits for a small group of elite shareholders rather than the welfare of the working majority. Worker self-directed enterprises are not nonprofits (which are often just as hierarchically structured as for-profit businesses and do not necessarily allow for broad-based agency). Instead, profits accrue to all who work in productive and reproductive capacities, along with the empowerment of all who work, thus benefiting the wider community rather than the few. Such efforts do not belong to the realm of theory alone, as there are growing networks of worker cooperatives in the United States and around the world, including a long and substantial history of cooperatives in African American communities in the United States.[59] Such

---

58 Richard D. Wolff, *Democracy at Work: A Cure for Capitalism* (Chicago: Haymarket Books, 2012).

59 Jessica Gordon Nembhard, *Collective Courage: A History of African American Cooperative Economic Development and Practice* (University Park: Pennsylvania State University Press, 2014). See also the work of the US Federation for Worker Cooperatives, https://www.usworker.coop/about/.

worker cooperatives provide fundamental alternatives to the way the economy functions in the Capitalocene, with significant implications for politics, culture, and religion providing alternatives to ecological destruction.

Ecological concerns are central in this alternative economic model in another way as well because, according to Schor, the basic principles of the new economy are the reduction of production and consumption (i.e., working less and spending less) and creating and connecting more—the latter possibility being enhanced by new communication technologies. In this context, Schor talks about "true materialism," which develops a new appreciation for things material and pushes beyond dominant materialisms that are interested in material things primarily for symbolic qualities.[60] Such true materialism is directly linked to providing opportunities for economically struggling communities. In theology, materialism is currently being reclaimed as well based on an understanding that the Abrahamic religions share a strong concern for the flourishing of life on this earth.[61] In fact, in most of the ancient Jewish traditions, the idea of salvation is not about going to heaven after death but about leading a happy and productive life, and several Christian traditions have been inspired by this.[62]

---

60 Schor and Thompson, "Introduction," 10, 13; see also Juliet B. Schor, *Plenitude: The New Economics of True Wealth* (New York: Penguin, 2010). See also Rieger, *No Rising Tide*, chap. 4.

61 See the reflections in chap. 2 of this book as well as Joerg Rieger and Edward Waggoner, eds., *Religious Experience and New Materialism: Movement Matters* (New York: Palgrave Macmillan, 2016).

62 For relevant Christian traditions, see, for instance, the so-called holiness movements. The founder of Methodism, John Wesley, makes a strong effort to tie salvation to what I tend to call "life before death," without dismissing, of course, life after death. See his

Models that draw their cues from emergent ecological thinking can also develop a deeper appreciation of diversity and difference. While diversity and difference can be employed to the benefit of neoliberal capitalism—diversifying production and consumption by employing a diversified (and therefore often cheaper) workforce and marketing and selling to nontraditional customers—things change when working people reclaim diversity and difference for their own interests. The result is alternative economies based on alternative production/reproduction and consumption patterns, embodied, for instance, in the growing number of networks forged between worker and consumer cooperatives. In this context, the capitalist drive for production and productivity is fundamentally transformed. Placing concerns for EM in this context could be promising, as it would fundamentally reshape the thrust and the meaning of modernization.

These new ways of accounting for diversity and difference also account for new forms of resilience and adaptability, along with a different kind of efficiency. In this way, diversity undergirds what Schor and Thompson have called a "networked revolution" and what, with Kwok Pui-lan and Rosemarie Henkel-Rieger, I have called "deep solidarity."[63] Deep solidarity is based on the collective agency of working people in contexts of exploitation, not only appreciating but putting to work differences and diversity along the lines of

---

sermon "The Scripture Way of Salvation," in *The Works of John Wesley*, ed. Albert C. Outler, vol. 2, the Bicentennial Edition (Nashville: Abingdon, 1985), 153–69.

63 Schor and Thompson, "Introduction," 22. Networks were, for instance, not yet on the horizon in Ernst F. Schumacher's *Small Is Beautiful*. For the term *deep solidarity*, see Rieger and Henkel-Rieger, *Unified*; and Rieger and Kwok, *Occupy Religion*.

race, ethnicity, gender, and sexuality in a constructive fashion. This creates alternatives to dominant models of solidarity that emphasize unity to the exclusion of diversity (see chapter 4).

Journalist Naomi Klein has also made an argument for the formation of networks of resistance, drawing connections between seemingly disparate struggles because "the logic that would cut pensions, food stamps, and health care before increasing taxes on the rich is the same logic that would blast the bedrock of the earth to get the last vapors of gas and the last drops of oil."[64] This serves as one more reminder of why economics is so crucial when discussing large-scale ecological destruction and climate change. While conservatives have long used economic arguments to stop climate action, Klein challenges progressives to use economic arguments in order to fight climate change.[65] Ignoring fundamental economic transformation because some experts feel this might be unrealistic turns out to be the one option that is actually unrealistic: hoping that things will fundamentally change without fundamentally changing the roots of the problem equates to an often-quoted definition of mental disorder attributed to Albert Einstein.[66] If climate change is indeed a matter of survival, it needs to be addressed by all means possible.

The perspective of ecologically informed economics also broadens the sense of importance of the resistance that is building. Opposition to fracking or high-risk pipelines, for

---

64   Naomi Klein, *This Changes Everything: Capitalism vs. the Climate* (New York: Simon & Schuster, 2015), 61.

65   Klein, 125.

66   "Doing the same thing over and over again and expecting a different result."

instance, is not merely a matter of environmental concern but also a matter of participation in the decision-making process in both politics and economics, as Klein has noted.[67] This opposition embodies the meaning of deep solidarity by being intersectional, interracial, and intergenerational, uniting people at the local level as well as at the global. Like some progressive theologians of the present, Klein finds hope in social movements that address the unfinished business of the liberation movements of the past two centuries, noting that victories on the legal (and we might add political and even religious) front were mostly lost on the economic front.[68]

The good news is that the utter urgency of climate change provides some fresh energy. In a reversal of Klein's account of the so-called shock doctrine, the impending disasters can be used not merely to advance the status quo but to add urgency and move us beyond easily ignored appeals to ethics and morality as the primary motivation.[69] This matches some of the underlying sensitivities of liberation theologies, where God-talk is focused not so much on ethics and morality (a widespread misunderstanding not only in theological circles) but on the energy of broader economic, social, and cultural-religious developments that push toward liberation. In other words, God is found not first of all in the world of ideas but in the tensions of life where alternative forms of production, reproduction, and agency—human and nonhuman—are emerging. This matches the experiences

---

67 Klein, *This Changes Everything*, 295.

68 Klein, 458. See also Rieger and Kwok, *Occupy Religion*.

69 See Naomi Klein, *The Shock Doctrine: The Rise of Disaster Capitalism* (New York: Picador, 2007); and Klein, *This Changes Everything*, 406, 417.

of figures revered in the Abrahamic religions like Moses, Jesus,[70] and Mohammed, but it can also be observed in the lives of grassroots religious communities through time, like the Franciscans, the Anabaptists of the sixteenth-century Reformation, the early Methodists, the African American slave communities, and the base ecclesial communities in Latin America.

Klein is right that solidarity is not an abstract moral ideal but built into the resistance to climate change, because today we are less isolated than a decade ago. The beginnings of such solidarity are already embodied in worker co-ops, farmer's markets, neighborhood sharing banks, and even to some degree social media.[71] Let us not forget that solidarity also shapes up in the agency of working people in concert with the planet and that a growing sense of solidarity is emerging in theology as well, pushing beyond certain limits of identity politics that have resulted in keeping people in silos for the time being (see chapter 4).[72]

---

70 For an excellent proposal to do ecological theology in terms of a "Christology from below" instead of the more common "cosmic Christ" approach, see T. Wilson Dickinson, *The Green Good News: Christ's Path to Sustainable and Joyful Life* (Eugene, OR: Cascade Books, 2019). Dickinson sees the problems of wealth and empire as central (xii). For a reading of the incarnation of Jesus along similar lines, including economic and ecological perspectives, see Celia Deane-Drummond, "Who on Earth Is Jesus Christ? Plumbing the Depths of Deep Incarnation," in *Christian Faith and the Earth: Current Paths and Emerging Horizons in Ecotheology*, ed. Ernst M. Conradie et al. (London: Bloomsbury T&T Clark, 2014).

71 Klein, *This Changes Everything*, 466.

72 One example is the experience of the Class, Religion, and Theology Unit at the American Academy of Religion. This group has been heavily engaged in cosponsoring sessions with groups that work on topics of race, ethnicity, gender, and culture.

Conclusions

In the fight against ecological destruction and climate change, a good deal of synergy emerges between ecology, economics, and theology. What has been part of the problem, it seems, can also become part of the solution. This takes us back to the fundamental problems in both economics and theology with which this chapter began.

Theological approaches can add a critique of economics that pushes beyond the approaches of environmental sociologists and economists, which could be useful in further conversations about ecology. Parallel to White's critique of Christianity as disconnected from nonhuman nature, there is broad agreement that capitalist economics throughout its history has been disconnected as well, both from nonhuman nature and from people. Things are only getting worse in neoliberal capitalism. As economist Robert Nelson has observed, the task of top neoliberal economists is to keep the big ideas of neoliberalism before people, with little concern for empirical studies and for analyzing data. In this way, he argues, economics comes to resemble a kind of religion that is also mostly about disembodied ideas.[73] This kind of religion is also characteristic of much of North Atlantic Christianity, which may be the reason why neoliberal economics and conservative Christianity display certain affinities, like faith in an intangible future and a firm belief in the work

---

73 Robert H. Nelson, *Economics as Religion: From Samuelson to Chicago and Beyond* (University Park: Pennsylvania State University Press, 2001). See also the critique of economics in Rieger, *No Rising Tide*.

of divine providence at work in capitalism no matter how severe its failures are.

However, things do not need to be this way, and alternatives already exist: instead of promoting disembodied ideas (that have too often not materialized for very long, and sometimes never), economics can be reconstructed from the ground up, in touch with the ecological, sociological, and political dynamics described in this chapter. The same is true for religion and theology. Instead of relegating itself to the promotion of disembodied ideas and troubling images of the divine that have done and continue to do tremendous damage (keep in mind that much resistance against climate science is currently supported in the name of religion), religion and theology can also be reconstructed from the ground up. Unexpected experiences of the divine involved in alternative ways of being in the material world and in communities—particularly in struggles for survival and flourishing, production and reproduction—are motivating people not only to resist but also to engage in alternative ways of life.

The theological battle is thus fought not merely about ideas and images of the divine but also about engagements with the divine in places where life is promoted, be it in nonhuman nature's resilience or in people's resistance and production of alternatives. Similar challenges can be posed to the academy as a whole: What if the major task is neither the formulation of big ideas—the perennial dream not only of religion but of many of the humanities—nor its opposite, the seemingly neutral collection of data, the proliferation of descriptive empirical studies, or technocratic solutions, but the engagement with emerging levels of resistance to the status quo and the concomitant forms of productivity and agency, both human and nonhuman, that mark our age?

2

The Immanence and Transcendence of Christianity and Capitalism

Alternatives to Ecological Devastation

Western Christianity has often been suspected of being a major contributor to the rampant ecological devastation that marks our age, if not its cause. While some see the problem with Christianity's anthropocentrism, playing off humanity and the earth and leading to the devaluation and destruction of the latter on a grand scale discussed in the previous chapter, others find fault with Western Christianity's emphasis on the nonmaterial, ethereal, and transcendent. In response to the latter problem, scholars of religion and theology have sought to give more prominent voice to religious traditions that emphasize the material, nonethereal, and immanent. Yet while religions that value the material and immanent over the immaterial and transcendent might seem to be poised to promote healthier concerns for the environment, this is not necessarily the case.

The so-called gospel of prosperity may serve as one example. Its celebration of wealth at the top—whether the wealth of its pastors or other prominent members of the community—not only lacks ecological concern but does little to alleviate the burdens imposed on the environment. The private jets of its most notorious representatives symbolize an interest in the material and immanent that is not only ecologically unsustainable but also hardly in reach of the masses. Seeking to imitate this kind of economic success, most of the followers of the gospel of prosperity fail while further damaging both their communities and the environment.

Capitalism, of course, serves as the primary example of how dominant concerns for material wealth and the immanent not only fail to protect the environment but are directly implicated in its exploitation, extraction, and destruction. In this context, valuing things material even more highly—for instance, through well-meaning efforts to shift the natural environment from an externality to a more integral part of capitalist economic calculations—may bring some relief, but it does not change the fact that the main goal of capitalist economics remains turning a profit (for the few) rather than saving the planet (for the many).

Religion, Immanence, and the Material

For those who find themselves drowning in oceans of religious, political, academic, and sometimes even economic idealism, engaging the value of immanence and material reality provides some relief. Such engagement needs to waste no time with the crude materialisms that rule the day in certain discourses of the natural sciences or with now mostly discredited reductionist economic determinisms. Reductionist accounts are of little help in developing the bigger picture we need.[1]

Against the backdrop of materialist reductionism, the current discussions emerging in the so-called new materialisms appear to be more fruitful. At stake is no longer the abortive discussion of whether "material" or "ideal" factors are all-determinative; the question is not even which factors are primary and secondary but how these factors influence and shape one another. In this way, new materialisms reclaim aspects of the more traditional historical and dialectical materialisms. Moreover, new materialisms can contribute to a constructive rethinking of religion, how it intersects with and is part of material reality, and what difference it makes. In addition, new materialisms also invite analyses of the existence of alternative religious practices that do not conform to the dominant powers, providing deeper investigations of their nature and promise.

In this spirit, new materialist religion scholars Clayton Crockett and Jeffrey Robbins reclaim Ludwig Feuerbach's materialist critique of religion with a positive twist: that human concerns play a major role in the formation of religion, they note, is reason not for rejecting religion but for

---

1   For a brief engagement with these materialisms, see Joerg Rieger, "Why Movements Matter Most: Rethinking the New Materialism for Religion and Theology," in Rieger and Waggoner, *Religious Experience*, 135–56.

reclaiming it.[2] New materialist scholars of religion invite the fields of religious studies and theology to take more seriously material and physical realities and to reconceive the roles of ecology, energy, and even economics in the production of religious experience. In the words of Crockett, "Materialism is not about the smallest building blocks of nature, whether atoms or quarks or strings, but the energetic transformation of reality by means of physical, chemical, biological, psychological, and social interactions."[3] While this increased concern for the material does not mean that material religion necessarily works for the good, in these accounts religion can be examined for its potential to become a force for empowerment and social change.

Such broadening of older materialist traditions is promising for various reasons. First, material revaluations of religion resonate with many of the Jewish traditions that have shaped and continue to shape Christianity. It has often been observed that salvation in the ancient Hebrew traditions is not about going to heaven after death but about the flourishing of life in the present. God's promise to Moses and the Hebrew slaves is not that their souls will live forever in heaven but that they will be liberated from slavery and will be led into a land flowing with milk and honey (Exod 3:7–10). What many nineteenth-century Western

---

2 Clayton Crockett and Jeffrey Robbins, *Religion, Politics, and the Earth: The New Materialism* (New York: Palgrave Macmillan, 2012), 18.

3 Clayton Crockett, "Plasticity and Change: Rethinking Difference and Identity with Catherine Malabou," in *Ecological Solidarities: Mobilizing Faith and Justice for an Entangled World*, ed. Krista E. Hughes, Dhawn Martin, and Elaine Padilla (University Park: Pennsylvania State University Press, 2019), 174. See also the chapters in Rieger and Waggoner, *Religious Experience*.

interpreters rejected as the primitive spirit of Judaism in comparison with Christianity—focusing on the concerns of the immanent rather than the transcendent—is now being reclaimed and valued again.

Second, reevaluating religion in immanent and material terms opens the view for a wealth of new insights produced by the natural sciences, from quantum physics and genetics to neurobiology. The natural sciences have come a long way from the days of Newtonian physics, when cause and effect, subject and object were easily distinguished and every question had a straightforward answer. This does not mean, however, that the natural sciences are beyond challenge and question. As the sciences are taken more seriously in the humanities and religious studies, keep in mind that "sciences (and technologies) and their societies co-constitute each other," as Sandra Harding has pointed out from a feminist and postcolonial perspective.[4] In other words, this new focus on immanence is complex, composed of various embodiments of immanence—natural and social ones—including the "superstructures" of both science and society.

Third, new materialisms reshape and broaden our understanding of human agency, which does not need to be understood as originating in transcendent ideas or good intentions. Noting a "mismatch between actions, intentions, and consequences," new materialists Diana Coole and Samantha Frost advocate an open systems approach when considering interactions between socioeconomic and

---

4 Sandra G. Harding, "Introduction: Beyond Postcolonial Theory; Two Undertheorized Perspectives on Science and Technology," in *The Postcolonial Science and Technology Studies Reader*, ed. Sandra G. Harding (Durham, NC: Duke University Press, 2011), 21.

environmental conditions, combining biological, physiological, and physical processes. By the same token, matter can be seen as having agency in its own right, as new materialists emphasize "the productivity and resilience of matter."[5] Matter is, therefore, always in a process of becoming rather than merely being. The same can be said, of course, of whatever is considered nature or the nonhuman environment. A great advantage of these approaches is that the possibility of transformation does not depend on the intentions of well-meaning individuals, and neither does it hinge primarily on the ideas of philosophers, theologians, or preachers.

New materialism thus offers some inspiration for rethinking both the immanent and the transcendent, although further clarity is needed about who the agents are and how alternative agency can emerge under the conditions of neoliberal capitalism, which seeks to harness every form of agency for its own purposes, human as well as nonhuman. A broadened analysis of capitalism appropriate to this task recognizes that (in the words of new materialists Coole and Frost) "the capitalist system is not understood in any narrowly economistic way but rather is treated as a detotalized totality that includes a multitude of interconnected phenomena and processes."[6] This brings us back to the overarching question that the social and ecological challenges of our age pose to us and with which this volume began: "What are we up against?"

---

5   Diana Coole and Samantha Frost, "Introducing the New Materialisms," in *New Materialisms: Ontology, Agency, Politics*, ed. Diana Coole and Samantha Frost (Durham, NC: Duke University Press, 2010), 7.

6   Coole and Frost, 29.

One approach to this question might be Coole and Frost's emphasis—not as dated as it might appear at first sight—on the "immense and immediate material hardship for real individuals" who lost their savings, their pensions, their houses, and their jobs in the meltdown of the economy after the Great Recession of 2007–9.[7] In the aftermath of the Covid-19 pandemic, which caused a short-lived economic crash followed by tremendous economic gains for the wealthiest Americans, so many Americans are struggling that one might talk about another sort of recession happening under the surface. Most of the jobs that were created in the wake of the Great Recession were not of the same quality as the jobs that were lost, with fewer benefits, lower compensation, and reduced influence and power at work, and the same is true once again for post-Covid-19 jobs. Reevaluating increasing ecological destruction and spiraling climate change in this light puts a new focus on conversations about ecology, as the most fundamental challenges are not anthropocentrism, an overemphasis of transcendence, or even a lack of concern for the immanent; they are the structures of neoliberal capitalism.

Reclaiming immanence without qualification, as in much of liberal theology, therefore, is not necessarily a solution but might be part of the problem. As Latin American liberation theologians pointed out decades ago, the immanence of dominant liberal middle-class theology that ruled much of the twentieth century and remains popular in the

---

7 Coole and Frost, 31.

twenty-first is not the immanence of oppressed and exploited people struggling for their liberation.[8]

Regrounding the Immanent and the Material

Basic analyses of the economy and of the tensions of social class (examined in greater detail in chapter 3) can help deepen conversations about the immanent and the material, although even some critics of capitalism seem to have lost sight of the issue. Current responses to financial capitalism, especially by theologians, have argued that all that matters in neoliberal capitalism is money and finance and that the market is now the transcendent—God.[9] While these arguments capture some aspects of what is going on, they overlook that material production and reproduction still play significant roles in capitalism's ultimate goal of increasing wealth. Why else would capitalism keep devouring both human and nonhuman natural resources in ever more dramatic fashion? Capitalism cannot indefinitely increase wealth (the wealth of the shareholders, to be sure) without increasing production, even if production is not always of material things, like the production of services and software and the reproduction of human existence that includes nurture and education.

---

8 Gustavo Gutiérrez, "The Limitations of Modern Theology: On a Letter of Dietrich Bonhoeffer," in *The Power of the Poor in History: Selected Writings* (Eugene, OR: Wipf & Stock, 2004), 222–34.

9 See, for instance, Kathryn Tanner, *The New Spirit of Capitalism* (New Haven, CT: Yale University Press, 2019); and Harvey Cox, *The Market as God* (Cambridge, MA: Harvard University Press, 2016).

What is at the heart of the ecological devastations of our age is, therefore, both immanent and transcendent, material and immaterial, and all are shaped by the dynamics of capitalism, which is why it makes more sense to talk about the Capitalocene than the Anthropocene (see chapter 1). While religion is a strong contender in this story of destruction as well, religion in its most damaging forms—for both people and the planet—has been aggressively reshaped by the interests of big money, particularly in the more recent history of the United States since the 1930s.[10] To be sure, there are many historical precedents, like early Christianity being pulled ever more closely in the orbit of the Roman Empire and reshaped to serve the dominant interests. What matters for the development of our argument, however, are not generic assertions that empires by definition seek to control everything, including religion. What matters is the particular history of capitalism and religion and its implications for particular forms of exploitation that now reach to the ends of the earth and beyond.

While new materialists tend to operate with a stronger sense of the impacts of capitalism than scholars of religion, a more substantial assessment of neoliberal capitalist reality is needed. The historical analyses of older materialisms—for instance, in various Marxist traditions—point the way by paying attention to the systematic exploitation of working people. The world of labor and production (both human and nonhuman) is where capitalism is rooted and where some of

---

10 For the history, see Kevin M. Kruse, *One Nation under God: How Corporate America Invented Christian America* (New York: Basic Books, 2015).

its greatest contradictions continue to manifest themselves. It is no accident that the pushback against working people and their associations (labor unions, organized communities, etc.) has been getting progressively worse, paralleled by the ever-growing exploitation of the environment.

If capitalism is thus built on the productive and reproductive labor of people and the planet, the world of production requires another look, not just in the study of economics, but also in the study of everything else, including matters of the environment and religion. Most important in this regard is the fact that production is not only the place of exploitation but also the place of resistance. This is another insight historically developed in materialist reflection, often overlooked especially by scholars of religion and theology and many others who tend to confuse materialist approaches with determinism. Productive labor and reproductive labor are not only sites of exploitation but the sites where resistance, agency, and even the ability to think and believe differently are located. This observation is at the very core of the argument of this book.

It is surprising, therefore, that even new materialisms hardly mention labor or work, mirroring the absence of the topic in the study of religion and theology. When labor is mentioned at all in one collection of essays that represents the spectrum of new materialisms, it is merely to make the point that new materialisms should go beyond the focus on labor that has been characteristic of materialisms in the past. But that hardly seems to be the problem today. Rosi Braidotti, a leading materialist feminist, develops her proposals as if labor did not even exist, proposing instead a "biocentered egalitarianism" that "breaks the expectation of mutual reciprocity," concluding that we have to give up ideas of retaliation and compensation.[11] While retaliation and "tit for tat" may indeed not be the most productive ways of relating to others, giving up notions of compensation and reciprocity in the current climate (including the climate of climate change) cannot be an option for people who have to work for a living—the proverbial 99 percent.

In order to move forward, new materialists and scholars of religion and theology may need to take a step back. When Crockett and Robbins "posit earth as subject" (including "materiality, energy forces, layered strata, atmosphere and magnetosphere, enfolded forms of life"),[12] people who have to work for a living are oddly absent. Yet working people not only make up the majority of humanity; they are also the agents who are sustaining much of human life at present—think not only production and agriculture but also services and care. To be sure, this includes both productive and reproductive labor and contributions to what is considered both material and immaterial (as well as immanent and transcendent). This recognition would go a long way toward pushing beyond dominant discourses stretching from politics to economics and religion, where the assumption still

---

11 Rosi Braidotti, "The Politics of 'Life Itself' and New Ways of Dying," in Coole and Frost, *New Materialisms*, 214.

12 Crockett and Robbins, *Religion, Politics, and the Earth*, xx. This proposal ends up being surprisingly anthropocentric, as the authors argue that "the Earth becomes who it is through us if we have the foresight and courage to realize it" (110). "Us" appears to be humanity, with no specific reflection on who that might be, and it is not clear where "foresight" and "courage" have their roots. Later, the authors claim that "thinking is an emergent property that issues from a brain" (127).

rules that Caesar built the Roman Empire, Henry Ford produced automobiles, Martin Luther King Jr. birthed the civil rights movement, and Paul singlehandedly expanded the early church's mission. Moreover, a closer look at the agency of the majority of humanity might throw new light on the agency of the nonhuman and help reclaim the revolutionary potential of both.

The parallels are worth noting: that which devalues the agency of the working majority (by cutting salaries, benefits, and hours at work; pushing employment at will; supporting the gig economy; and exploiting unpaid reproductive work) also devalues the agency of the nonhuman. Moreover, the capitalist exploitation of labor and nature presupposes a certain hierarchy of labor over nature, stemming from a reversal of the ancient primacy of the productivity of land to the productivity of labor.[13] In this framework, unpaid reproductive labor, typically performed by women in patriarchal societies, is equated with nonhuman nature, and the same is true for the unpaid labor of enslaved people, whose numbers are higher than ever before in history.[14] Yet while unpaid reproductive labor, both human and nonhuman, is pushed lower than productive labor, it is the sine qua non of production, as the productivity of labor absolutely depends on it.

---

13 Moore, "Rise of Cheap Nature," 91.

14 For slavery today, see Kevin Bales, *Blood and Earth: Modern Slavery, Ecocide, and the Secret to Saving the World* (New York: Spiegel & Grau, 2016). Bales estimates that globally, there are 35.8 million slaves today (9). Bales also notes the ecological destruction that goes hand in hand with the practice of slavery, as slaveholders are behind some of the most destructive mining practices and the clear-cutting of forests, putting their combined CO_2 output in third place, behind the United States and China (10).

Moreover, it can be argued that without reproductive labor, life as such could not exist (see below, chapter 3).

Capitalism's efforts to downplay both productive and reproductive labor are mirrored in the histories of religion and theology. The agency of working people is still mostly relegated to a footnote, even in many theologies that consider themselves liberative. And even where some of this agency is studied, this is often done without understanding its importance for the development of religion as a whole. The study of popular religion, for instance, tends to study popular religious experience in itself, in isolation from dominant religious experience. In Christian theology, to give another example, Jesus preaching good news to the poor and uplifting them is noted often without linking it to the emerging agency of the people that poses a challenge to the powers that be. In Jesus's imagination, by contrast, even the stones can be agents of resistance against the forces of the empire (Luke 19:40).

Karl Marx's critique of Ludwig Feuerbach's materialism is instructive here because it highlights the agency of labor. Going beyond Feuerbach, Marx observes that material objects and matter itself are not mere givens but produced by labor and commerce, which means that materialism needs to take into account the produced nature of matter. Material reality, in other words, is never an entity in and of itself, as it is constantly produced and reproduced, including the reproductive labor performed by women, enslaved people, and nature, which is taken for granted even by some who are concerned with productive labor. Even the so-called natural world is impacted by this, as it has been shaped by human labor in some form or fashion. This fact did not escape

Marx, even though the human impact on nature was less pronounced in his time than today, as the European landscape had already been substantially transformed by the cutting down of forests, the extractive mining of coal, and various agricultural techniques. In all of this, human agency is inextricably tied up with the nonhuman agency of nature, as both nature and working people are constantly engaged in "changing the form of matter." This is where capitalism has its deepest roots, as wealth is generated from the interplay of labor and nature. In the words of Marx, "[Humans] can work only as Nature does, that is by changing the form of matter. Nay more, in this work of changing the form [they are] constantly helped by natural forces."[15]

While the new materialisms have broadened our understanding of the productive capacities of nature far beyond what Marx and his contemporaries could have imagined, the interaction of labor and nature needs further investigation. In this quest, a deeper analysis of the fundamental—and therefore potentially revolutionary—contributions of human labor (both productive and reproductive) might guide the way.

Economic Democracy Reclaiming Immanence and Transcendence

As we deepen these materialist intuitions, the tasks of the study of religion and theology are being redefined. Instead of studying disembodied ideas and seemingly universal truths,

---

15   Karl Marx, *Capital: A Critique of Political Economy*, vol. 1, bk. 1, trans. Samuel Moore and Edward Aveling, ed. Frederick Engels (Moscow: Progress, 1887), https://www.marxists.org/archive/marx/works/download/pdf/Capital-Volume-I.pdf.

the task is now to study material relations and the respective ideas that are produced and reproduced in the context of particular relations of power. We might call this the labor of religion, which develops in relation to productive and reproductive labor performed by working people, who make up the majority of humanity (the proverbial 99 percent).

At stake is more than a methodological issue. Scholars of religion and theology will not be able to recognize alternative forms of religion unless they take into account the history of how power is shaped and reshaped in particular material social relations and social movements. As a result, we need to pay closer attention to whose agency matters in what ways and who benefits and who does not in a given system—keeping in mind the agency of both people and nature. This question of agency is at the core of all democratic traditions: Who is calling the shots, who is in charge, who embodies power? These questions push beyond political democracy, which in modern nations is typically identified either with casting ballots in the voting booth or with the politics of protest or social movements.

Reclaiming materialist traditions allows us to broaden our notions of democracy to include economic and labor relations on the one hand and religion and other cultural productions on the other. Why should the rule of people be limited to the political realm, whether defined as party politics or, broadly, as matters of public interest? Why should places of work, where people spend the single biggest block of time each week, be exempt from the principles of democracy? Why should people's productive and reproductive activities at work be discounted from influencing the social and ecological changes we so desperately need? And why not include religion and culture in conversations about democracy?

The fundamental question of economic democracy is, How do we harness alternative powers that are already at work on the ground but commonly overlooked even by those who seek to organize and reorganize political democracy? Moreover, how do we push beyond elitist notions of democracy that we have inherited from our Western traditions, according to which the primary agents are those who have the leisure and the time to engage in political activities? While we have arrived at a system of universal suffrage for all citizens in the United States, in contrast to the elitist politics of the Greek polis and early forms of US democracy, the actual political agency of most people is still fairly limited. When a Jeff Bezos or an Elon Musk, now the wealthiest individuals in the world, pick up the phone to call a US senator or the governor of a state, they will get a different response than any number of ordinary citizens. Economic democracy might help remedy that.

Furthermore, economic democracy includes the nonhuman, but less abstractly than in many new materialist discourses. Already Marx understood what sociologists Brett Clark and Richard York have called the "metabolic interaction" between humanity and the earth, noting that "man lives on nature," so that "nature is his body, with which he must remain in continuous interchange if he is not to die."[16]

---

16 Clark and York, "Carbon Metabolism," 398. The metabolic rift (John Bellamy Foster) is created by capitalism, for instance, when nutrients are not returned to the soil because they are shipped to cities, where they are creating a waste problem.

In other words, what is often considered the nonhuman is an inextricable part of humanity, and capitalist destruction affects everything, as an increasing number of studies show.[17]

Two conclusions follow from this: First, taking a closer look at economic democracy in relation to productive and reproductive labor will help us become more aware of the produced nature of everything that surrounds us, including politics, religious practice, and even the nonhuman environment. Discovering the produced nature of everything does not imply a negative judgment, as being produced does not mean to be of lesser importance; it simply reminds us of the fact that nothing ever just "fell from the sky," not even religion or nature, and—this is the point most important to my argument—that there may be alternative modes of production that can be explored and harnessed for transformation.

Second, a closer look at economic democracy in relation to production reveals its complexity, as production is both material and immaterial with implications for both immanence and transcendence. There is, for instance, an odd sort of transcendence that occurs when produced objects are commodified. Marx uses the example of a table. In terms of its use value, there is nothing mysterious about a table. Wood, produced by nature, is transformed by human labor into a common thing to be used for particular purposes: a dining-room table, a desk, a kitchen table, and so on. A

---

17 It is rarely noted that already Marx himself understood these connections and incorporated them into his critique of capitalism. John Bellamy Foster, *Marx's Ecology: Materialism and Nature* (New York: Monthly Review Press, 2000), is the pioneering book on this topic. For a fresh reading of Marx along these lines, see Kohei Saito, *Karl Marx's Ecosocialism: Capital, Nature, and the Unfinished Critique of Political Economy* (New York: Monthly Review Press, 2017).

certain kind of transcendence enters in terms of the exchange value of the table. In capitalist economies, the table becomes a commodity, and what matters is no longer the labor, the materials, or even its use value but the profit that can be made when this table is sold. But because profit is usually thought of as a relationship between things, what is concealed is that it is actually produced in a relationship between people—in other words, the question of economic democracy.[18] In Marx's own words, under the conditions of capitalism, "a commodity is therefore a mysterious thing, simply because in it the social character of men's labour appears to them as an objective character stamped upon the product of that labour; because the relation of the producers to the sum total of their own labour is presented to them as a social relation, existing not between themselves, but between the products of their labour."[19] Marx compares this to religious ideas, where "the productions of the human brain appear as independent beings endowed with life."[20] What happens when the material and immaterial are made visible in these seemingly mundane processes of everyday labor, and what alternatives might emerge?

Keep in mind that even when the significance of labor and democratic human relationships is concealed by the capitalist dynamics of commodification (which then leads to commodity fetishism), labor and human relationships

---

18　Marx talks about these issues in *Capital*, but since he does not mention the terms *exchange value* and *profit* in this section, it is difficult to follow. Karl Marx, *A Critique of Political Economy*, trans. Ben Fowkes, vol. 1 of *Capital* (London: Penguin Classics, 1976), 46–47.

19　Marx, 46–47.

20　Marx, 47.

remain fundamental. Sara Ahmed, another new materialist thinker, adds an important insight that extends production and labor to reproductive labor and broadens our reflections on economic democracy: the example of the table points to other divisions of labor, manifest, for instance, in the division between who usually works at desks and who usually works at kitchen tables. In this example, the kitchen table represents the racial, gender, and class-based divisions of labor, as desk work is often supported by the domestic labor of Black and working-class women.[21] Moreover, reproductive human labor is often valued less—like the labor of nonhuman nature—and considered to be a so-called externality that is either unpaid and taken for granted or pushed to the very bottom of the ranks of production. Literary scholar Daniel Hartley has highlighted the important role that culture plays here: "If women's work has been historically vital to capitalism, then we must conclude . . . that culture is more than a force of ideological *legitimation*, it is itself a materially *constitutive* and *productive* moment in capitalist value relations."[22] In other words, a deeper investigation of work and economic democracy does not need to sacrifice the concerns of race, gender, and sexuality to the concerns of class; it reminds us of the importance of all of these concerns to ecology and ultimately to theology!

Observing labor relations in terms of economic democracy matters not only for analytical purposes but also for a determination of what kinds of alternatives might emerge

---

21 Sara Ahmed, "Orientations Matter," in Coole and Frost, *New Materialisms*, 248–54.

22 Daniel Hartley, "Anthropocene, Capitalocene, and the Problem of Culture," in Moore, *Anthropocene or Capitalocene?*, 162.

from specific labor situations, both material and immaterial, immanent and transcendent. Economic democracy—embodied where most people spend the bulk of their waking hours and where most of their sustenance is anchored—has a tremendous impact on political democracy, whether we realize it or not. That so much of politics is determined either by people who enjoy the privilege of having agency at work (i.e., managers and bosses) or simply by economic prowess (i.e., large amounts of capital) is directly linked to the lack of economic democracy. Moreover, economic democracy has implications for not only political but also religious democracy: not only will religious practices and images of God developed by minority women of the working class be different; they also will provide much-needed challenges to dominant religious practices and images of God.

Jason Moore concisely formulates the task before us when he argues that "the organization of work—inside and outside the cash nexus, in all its gendered, semicolonial, and racialized forms—must be at the center of our explanations, and our politics."[23] This has implications not only for the study and practice of economics and politics but also for the study and practice of religion and theology: economic democracy, political democracy, and religious democracy are closely related and shape and reshape one another. At the core of it all is a relational view of power that emphasizes economic democracy and labor relations as essential, with substantial implications for ecological and environmental

---

23   Moore, "Rise of Cheap Nature," 93. Moore's argument that capitalism has been able to contain the rising costs of production by using nature's work as a cheap resource (114) is incomplete at best, as labor costs have also been kept low.

concerns. This parallels my repeated interventions regarding the study of class as relationship rather than stratification, to which we will return in chapter 3.[24]

Reshaping Transcendence and Immanence and the Study of Religion, Theology, and Ecology

The reflections so far can help reframe the options in the study of religion and theology and shape alternative approaches to ecology. What Marx calls religion in the above example is how philosophical idealists and many theologians view religion, as (seemingly) "independent beings endowed with life."[25] But there is no reason why religion cannot be defined differently, from a more materialist perspective that takes into account the relation of life to material realities. The same is true for the notion of transcendence: It does not have to be defined in reference to the world of ethereal ideas, the mind, or whatever might be beyond nature. Similarly, transcendence does not have to be determined by capitalism as either the transcendence of the commodity or the seemingly transcendent flow of money in financial capitalism disconnected for production and labor.

There are materialist ways to conceive of transcendence—for instance, when it is defined not in opposition to immanence but as transcending one kind of immanence in favor of another. This corresponds with the Jewish traditions,

---

24 To my knowledge, the notion of class as relationship rather than stratification has only been picked up very recently in religious studies. See Joerg Rieger, ed., *Religion, Theology, and Class: Fresh Engagements after Long Silence* (New York: Palgrave Macmillan, 2013).

25 Marx, *Critique of Political Economy*, 47.

where salvation is not about escaping to another world but about the flourishing of life here and now, as noted above. In Christianity, this is one way to understand the incarnation of Christ, where the Roman Empire is transcended not by ethereal ideas or otherworldly dreams proclaimed in sermons but by God's solidarity with the peasant movements with which the construction worker Jesus of Nazareth aligns himself. In this case, transcendence is what interrupts the status quo (an idea also expressed by the Jewish philosopher Emmanuel Levinas[26]) and that which is diametrically opposed to the status quo—totally other.

Such notions of transcendence are not as foreign to religion and theology as they might appear at first sight. The quintessential modern theologian of transcendence, Karl Barth, whose basic conversion from liberal theology to a more radical approach took place in close relation to the labor movement in Switzerland, realized that to confess "God in the highest" does not mean to look up to the sky or away to other worlds. Recalling the story of the birth of Christ in a stable in Bethlehem, Barth notes that this is the proper place of transcendence: "The highness of God consists in His thus descending."[27] This is the point of the Barthian notion of the divine as the wholly other—*der ganz Andere*. In contrast to the liberal-traditionalist tug-of-war between immanence and transcendence that still shapes so

---

26 Emmanuel Levinas, *Totality and Infinity: An Essay in Exteriority*, trans. Alphonso Lingis (Pittsburgh: Duquesne University Press, 1969).

27 Karl Barth, *Dogmatics in Outline* (New York: Harper & Row, 1959), 40. For the background of Barth's lifelong socialism, see George Hunsinger, ed., *Karl Barth and Radical Politics* (Philadelphia: Westminster, 1976), especially the contributions by Friedrich Wilhelm Marquardt and Helmut Gollwitzer.

much of theology today, the concepts of both transcendence and immanence are transformed here. Transcendence, we might conclude, is not the otherworldly or the supernatural but the alternative immanence that totally reshapes dominant immanence.

While capitalism needs to cover up this alternative immanence—the contributions of productive and reproductive labor (both human and nonhuman)—the study of religion can resist this cover-up by acknowledging labor (both human and nonhuman), thus reshaping whatever might be defined as its transcendent or transcending tasks. This has implications for ecology as well. At the core of my argument here is a fundamental shift of perspective that I have suggested earlier, when the Great Recession was in full swing: the shift from a focus on the widespread concern for the redistribution of wealth to the production of wealth.[28] While the common concern for the redistribution of wealth remains important in a time of rising inequality, it tends to overlook the roots of inequality and ecological destruction, which are located in how productive and reproductive labor are valued. If human and nonhuman labor engaged in production and reproduction were appreciated appropriately (rather than pushed out of sight and exploited), the distribution of wealth would be corrected as well. Many of the environmental injustices that we see today have their roots here, in the exploitation of productive and reproductive labor, from environmental racism to food injustice and the most extreme extraction of natural resources.

---

28   Rieger, *No Rising Tide.*

In conjunction with developing a new appreciation for human production and reproduction and its revolutionary potential, nonhuman production and reproduction can now also be seen in a new light. Rethinking the working majority as subjects in this way has the potential to illuminate notions of the earth as subject. Whitney Bauman's notion of "bio-histories"[29] could be helpful as we reevaluate the contributions of the planet and its agency. Note that this conversation pushes beyond the typical efforts of trying to appreciate the environment more or accounting for the environment in economic calculations; it is about becoming aware of and supporting new forms of the agency of nature that not only resist ecological destruction but bring forth new kinds of ecological flourishing that benefit both humans and nonhumans. The immanence that emerges here has transcendent qualities, as it fundamentally challenges and reshapes the immanence of the current status quo.

Theologians might think of images of Gaia (both in ancient and contemporary conversations) and proclamations of the earth as God's body (Sallie McFague), but it might be more helpful to think about the earth's agency in more specific terms related to productive and reproductive labor. This includes the production and reproduction of life at all levels, including the work of plants and animals; that the vast majority of vertebrates are now domesticated further points to the inextricable relation of human and nonhuman production and reproduction.[30] In other words, talking about the

---

29 Bauman, *Religion and Ecology*, 165.
30 In terms of vertebrates, wild animals account only for 3 percent of the total mass (in weight), humans account for 30 percent, and domesticated animals account for

earth, the nonhuman, and transcendence in this perspective is not primarily about finding metaphysical inspiration in a sunset or a walk in the park; the transcendence of the earth and of the nonhuman is about agency that counters ecological destruction and creates new possibilities for the flourishing of life. An example from the world of undomesticated animals made the rounds during the raging wildfires in Australia in late 2019 and early 2020, where wombats shared their burrows with animals escaping certain death. As the myth had it, these wombats would actively shepherd other animals into their burrows to protect them, but such strong notions of agency are not necessary—the act of sharing itself is remarkable and appears to be a common way of life for wombats rather than some extraordinary action reserved for catastrophes.[31] Of course, it is now understood that even wildfires have some agency that can allow for the flourishing of new life. Such reflections on nonhuman agency might inspire conversations about what might be called ecological democracy in addition to economic democracy, but we cannot pursue them here.

Talking about production and reproduction in this way transcends activities determined by processes of production and reproduction under the conditions of capitalism. The conversation needs to include, as Jason Edwards suggests, "all those practices involving material bodies—organic and

---

67 percent. See Bill McKibben, *Falter: Has the Human Game Begun to Play Itself Out?* (New York: Henry Holt, 2019), 12.

31 See Sara Barnes, "Viral Posts Claim Wombats Are Shepherding Animals to Their Burrows during Australian Bushfires," My Modern Met, January 15, 2020, https://mymodernmet.com/viral-wombat-post-australia-bushfires/.

nonorganic—that . . . can be seen as a totality of practices that reproduce the relations of production over time."[32] This is an important reminder not only regarding nonhuman agency; human labor also needs to be seen in a broader light. At a time when labor is shifting and more and more people are pushed into the informal sectors of the economy— into casual jobs in the gig economy, temp jobs, or no formal employment at all—production itself needs to be rethought in terms of both its problems and its promises. This includes reproductive labor and any kind of work currently done without compensation, like volunteer work, housework, or even the gestational labor of women that is rarely valued to its fullest extent.[33] What Edwards calls "the constitution of experience through the manifold forms of material practice outside the immediate space of production"[34] needs to be considered as well. This also includes *lo cotidiano*, "the every-day," of which *Mujerista* theologian Ada María Isasi-Díaz used to remind scholars of theology and religion.[35] This brings a particular focus to the study of the immanent, and it transforms notions of what is considered transcendent, spiritual, and so on.[36]

---

32 Jason Edwards, "The Materialism of New Materialism," in Coole and Frost, *New Materialisms*, 283.

33 For a powerful reflection on gestational labor, see Elizabeth Freese, "The Christian Right's Main Moral Argument against Abortion Rights Ignores This Critical Issue: It's Time to Raise It," *Religion Dispatches*, May 7, 2021, https://religiondispatches.org/the-christian-rights-main-moral-argument-against-abortion-rights-completely-ignores-this-critical-issue-its-time-to-raise-it/.

34 Edwards, "Materialism of New Materialism," 288.

35 See, for instance, Ada María Isasi-Díaz, *Mujerista Theology: A Theology for the Twenty-First Century* (Maryknoll, NY: Orbis Books, 1996).

36 See the argument in Joerg Rieger, *Jesus vs. Caesar: For People Tired of Serving the Wrong God* (Nashville: Abingdon, 2018), chap. 3.

At stake is not merely the analysis of the impact of imminent and material practices on religion; it is also the potential that reshaping processes of production and reproduction might have for reshaping religious ideas, experience, and practice. This is not yet another utopian dream about life outside the dominant system—and it has even less to do with conventional understandings of transcendence. Even theologians might find themselves in cautious agreement with Edwards that "the material practices constitutive of modern life are the only grounds from which we could hope and expect to bring about important political and social transformations."[37] While material practices can and do make us compliant with the status quo—the world of productive and reproductive labor under the conditions of capitalism is designed to do exactly this—they also harbor the potential for resistance and for producing alternatives. This, then, is the place to start looking for transcendence again.

Which material practices are currently producing the most fertile ground for the alternative agency that is needed to transcend the exploitative relationships that affect both people and the earth? In the times of Jesus of Nazareth, the practices of peasants seem to have provided this ground; in Marx's time, it was industrial labor—what he called the proletariat. Today, that question is more complex—some would point to the so-called precariat, which includes not only people belonging to the traditional working class but all whose existence is precarious now, even once-proud professionals, managers, and university professors whose departments are

---

37 Edwards, "Materialism of New Materialism," 292.

eliminated.[38] But the question is not just who is affected by capitalism but also who has what it takes to resist, and so intersectional movements of working people (both formal and informal) need to be taken into account, including the nonhuman agency of the ecological environment that may well present one of the biggest challenges to capitalism yet because it can never be suppressed and controlled altogether.

Such an approach provides new clues for the study of religions like the Abrahamic ones, which originated among the working majorities in times of economic and political turmoil and continued to be shaped in part by the struggles of working people throughout their history.[39] These and other religious movements developed in close relationship to working people and the material practices and alternative ways of life and thought that grow out of them. This is also where considerable progress in the fight against sexism (according to the traditions of socialist feminism) and racism (according to Martin Luther King Jr., W. E. B. Du Bois, and many others[40]) has been made, and here is where progress in the fight against ecological destruction finds increasing support as well. At stake is not only the greening of the economy but

---

38 Guy Standing, *The Precariat: The New Dangerous Class* (London: Bloomsbury, 2011).

39 See Ulrich Duchrow and Franz Josef Hinkelammert, *Transcending Greedy Money: Interreligious Solidarity for Just Relations* (New York: Palgrave Macmillan, 2012); and Rieger and Henkel-Rieger, *Unified*.

40 See, for instance, the following statement by W. E. B. Du Bois, *Writings by W. E. B. Du Bois in Periodicals Edited by Others*, vol. 4, collated and ed. Herbert Aptheker (Millwood, NY: Kraus-Thomson Organization, 1982), 68: "Probably the greatest and most effective effort toward interracial understanding among the working masses has come about through the trade unions." Martin Luther King Jr., "Highlander Folk School, Monteagle, Tennessee, September 1957," in *All Labor Has Dignity*, ed. Michael K. Honey (Boston: Beacon, 2011), 14, put it this way: "Organized labor is one of the Negro's strongest allies in the struggle for freedom."

the specific nature of the green economy, including green jobs that not only pay fair wages but also give workers a say in what is happening at work and where they, rather than the stockholders, are able to appropriate the profits for the sake of their communities. This is where economic democracy finds its roots, eventually impacting political, cultural, and religious democracy as well.

In sum, as alternative religious subjectivities and practices emerge in the history of particular movements of exploited working people in touch with the agency of the exploited earth, not only do notions of immanence and transcendence change; notions of religion and theology change as well. Rather than trying to conjure up alternative religious subjectivities and practices out of thin air, scholars of religion and theology will have to study them while immersing themselves in the resistance movements of our time, exploring what all of this might mean for the future of religion, including its practices, its doctrines and beliefs, and its ways of life. To bring it down to a formula that may sound strange when pronounced at the level of the academic study of religion and theology, the confluence of materialism and religion needs movements, and it needs the movements of the working majority (formal and informal ones, self-organizing and cooperative) along with all the nonhuman movements of nature and the earth that new materialists have been exploring. This is democracy at work at ever-deeper levels—including economic and ecological ones—many of which we still have to explore.

Conclusions

At the heart of my argument are questions of power and agency: What are we up against, where are the contradictions, and what are the alternatives? Among the most basic contradictions in neoliberal capitalism are still exploitative and extractive relationships of productive labor. This is so despite the developments of financial capitalism and other seemingly ethereal processes that have led scholars to argue that economics functions like a religion (defined as abstract ideas hovering above everyday life; see previous chapter). These exploitative relationships of production are compounded (not merely augmented) by the extraction and exploitation of the reproductive labor of women, minorities, and nonhuman nature. The tensions produced in these increasingly contentious relationships (yes, class struggle is a reality, as Warren Buffett noted in 2006[41]) challenge the last pretenses of scholarly objectivity—the work of scholars of religion and theology cannot escape them, and so we need to decide what to do with them and how to rethink and reconstruct them.

In order to do that, scholars of theology and religion will need to revisit fundamental questions like immanence and transcendence, religion and capitalist economics, and ecological catastrophes such as climate change that threaten the future of human life on the planet. Since power and agency do not fall from the sky (another widespread misunderstanding

---

41 Ben Stein, "In Class Warfare, Guess Which Class Is Winning," *New York Times*, November 26, 2006, https://www.nytimes.com/2006/11/26/business/yourmoney/26every.html.

of transcendence), we will also need to investigate their formation and reformation in economic and ecological democracy and their embodiment in political, cultural, and religious forms of democracy.

In the meantime, there are already some explorations of how movements of working people, including women around the world and minority populations, shape and reshape ecological concerns, from community gardens to networks of worker cooperatives, with implications for the reshaping of political and religious concerns.[42] Is there anything else today that has the potential to transform the dominant status quo, both in its immanent and material functions on the ground as well as in its false promises of transcendence (to be the tide that lifts all boats, to make America great again, and to bring happiness and peace)?

---

[42] See, for instance, Ryan-Simkins and Nogueira-Godsey, "Tangible Actions toward Solidarity"; Gordon Nembhard, *Collective Courage*; and Schor and Thompson, *Sustainable Lifestyles*; see also chapter 3 below.

3

Class and Its Discontents in the Study of Religion and Theology

Reconfiguring Relationships and Power

For much of the twentieth century and for the first decades of the twenty-first, except for a brief interlude occasioned by the Occupy Wall Street movement, the topic of class has rarely been investigated. Even the Left has often given up on the notion of class, although some are currently rediscovering it, noting the irony that the disappearance of class coincides with neoliberal capitalism's march to victory.[1] While the notion of class has an established place in the often-referenced triad of race, gender, and class, the discussion of class is oddly underdeveloped compared to the

---

1   See, for instance, Vivek Chibber, *The Class Matrix: Social Theory after the Cultural Turn* (Cambridge, MA: Harvard University Press, 2022), 9–13.

other categories.[2] Even in US higher education, when critical reflection is still upheld as a value, students are more likely to study gender and race than class. In a volume that introduces intersectional theology, for instance, the glossary contains three separate entries related to gender, entries on race and sexism, but no entry on class.[3] Many of my students who bring up class analysis in other courses are actively discouraged from doing so. As legal scholar Joan Williams has put it, tongue in cheek, "Class consciousness has been replaced by class cluelessness."[4]

An even bigger problem is that assumptions about class persist, if only below the surface, and they often create more trouble for understanding class than they solve. Consciously or unconsciously, most Americans identify class with social stratification, according to income and wealth, educational

---

2 John Russo and Sherry Lee Linkon, "New Working Class Studies," in *New Working Class Studies*, ed. John Russo and Sherry Lee Linkon (Ithaca, NY: ILR, 2005), 3–5, make a similar case about American studies and studies along the lines of multiculturalism, which also focuses on race, gender, and class, increasingly including issues of sexuality. The common focus on race and gender at the expense of class transcends the academy and the context of the United States. When, in 1994, newly elected South African president Nelson Mandela publicly declared that freedom along the lines of race and gender was at the heart of the new South Africa, he left out class; "Inaugural Speech, Pretoria [Mandela]," University of Pennsylvania, African Studies Center, May 11, 1994, https://www.africa.upenn.edu/Articles_Gen/Inaugural_Speech_17984.html. The ongoing struggles of South Africa testify to the deeply problematic nature of this neglect of class, as class relationships remain foundational to South African society.

3 Grace Ji-Sun Kim and Susan M. Shaw, *Intersectional Theology: An Introductory Guide* (Minneapolis: Fortress, 2018). In the index, class is listed, but the passages in the text to which they refer mention class without ever defining it, usually in conjunction with lists of other markers of oppression. And while the text mentions "oppression" as well as "hurt, division, separation, and pain" (110), the term *exploitation* does not appear.

4 Joan C. Williams, *White Working Class: Overcoming Class Cluelessness in America* (Boston: Harvard Business Review Press, 2017), 2.

achievements,[5] social status,[6] cultural dispositions[7] (high-brow versus lowbrow), and so on, perhaps recalling some lessons from introductory sociology classes in high school or college.[8] Several of these definitions are combined in the example of a tenured professor at a prominent theological seminary who assumed that she was upper-middle class because of her PhD degree and professorial status but also working class, as she needed to stock shelves at a grocery store to make ends meet (she is not the only one in that inopportune position). Unfortunately, such definitions not only neglect some of the more interesting aspects of class but point class analysis in the wrong direction.

Stratification theories of class eschew relational understandings of class, particularly those that focus on the distortions of relationships between classes and the existence of power differentials that affect not only economics but also politics, culture, and religion. A cursory look at US politics exemplifies the lack of relational understanding of the realities of class and the predominance of stratification theories.

---

5 Tamara Draut, *Sleeping Giant: How the Working Class Will Transform America* (New York: Doubleday, 2016), defines the working class as anyone without a college degree.

6 The emphasis on social status typically follows the work of sociologist Max Weber.

7 Much is made of class cultures. Williams, *White Working Class*, 12, defines the so-called white working class in terms of "a cultural tradition that people riff off as they shape their everyday behavior and make sense of their lives." See also the various works of sociologist of religion Tex Sample, *Hard Living People & Mainstream Christians* (Nashville: Abingdon, 1993).

8 The concept of stratification has often gotten its authorization from the work of Weber, who analyzed class in terms of status, which includes income, wealth, occupation, and education. Yet as Kevin J. Christiano, William H. Swatos, and Peter Kivisto, *Sociology of Religion: Contemporary Developments*, 2nd ed. (Lanham, MD: Rowman & Littlefield, 2008), 133, point out, Weber might be understood as complementing and enriching Karl Marx's tradition at this point rather than opposing it. Unfortunately, the concept of stratification has often been used in this latter way.

In the run-up to the 2020 presidential elections, while most candidates of the Democratic Party were perceived as being supportive of working people, only Vermont senator Bernie Sanders touched on the relationship between working people and the proverbial one percent. Like most Democrats, Republican incumbent Donald Trump presented himself as a champion of working people, covering up class relationships in his own way by presenting one percenters as role models for success, as if they inhabited the upper social strata solely due to their individual merit and hard work.

Adding to the roadblocks to understanding class is the American infatuation with the middle class, which is mistakenly assumed to make up the majority of the population with a small section of wealthy elites at the top and a limited number of poor minorities at the bottom. In this mindset, the existence of an executive or ruling class is often neglected either because it seems statistically insignificant or because middle-class interests are considered more foundational.[9] Typical reflections on the middle class also exemplify the problem of emphasizing stratification rather than relationship. Stratification theories can make it look as if this middle class exists for itself in a place of relative comfort and ready privilege, occasionally becoming a stepping-stone upward or a trapdoor downward. In reality, middle-class life is more likely to resemble a battleground where the executive class recruits middle management, charged with controlling the

---

9   There is little awareness and virtually no study of this topic, although popular TV shows like *Billions* and *Succession* that display the lives of the extremely wealthy have a substantial following. Exceptions include quirky projects like Richard Conniff's *The Natural History of the Rich: A Field Guide* (New York: W. W. Norton, 2003).

working class. Compliance by the middle class can be motivated by confusing its own interests with those of the ruling class, by the growing fear of falling, or by US law that prohibits middle management from joining labor unions (unlike middle management in Europe and elsewhere). As Chinese scholar Li Chunling argues, "Middle class theory exists in the West to cover up the issue of class conflict."[10] For all these reasons, the US middle class has a hard time seeing itself in solidarity with what Jeremy Posadas calls the "invisible feet of the market."[11] As media studies professor Catherine Liu has pointed out, this lack of awareness of class creates major problems for academics even when they are committed to the cherished traditions of critical reflection in the humanities and social sciences or when they seek to take on what they consider to be causes of social transformation.[12]

A more sustained analysis of class and its discontents—without ignoring other forms of pressures along the lines of race, gender, and ecological destruction—can help address many of these misconceptions and contribute to the development of alternatives that have implications not only for the study of religion and theology but also for broader questions of academic study in various other fields. Rather than

---

10 Reference in Göran Therborn, "An Agenda for Class Analysis," *Catalyst* 3, no. 3 (2019): 105.

11 Jeremy Posadas, "The Invisible Feet of the Market," Institute for Christian Socialism, March 8, 2021, https://christiansocialism.com/invisible-feet/.

12 Catherine Liu, *Virtue Hoarders: The Case against the Professional Managerial Class* (Minneapolis: University of Minnesota Press, 2021), 1, describes the "professional managerial class" as considering itself "the heroes of history, fighting to defend innocent victims against their evil victimizers," but lending no support to the working class because "by PMC standards they do not behave properly: they are either disengaged politically or too angry to be civil."

playing off class and identity politics, this chapter prepares the ground for a conversation between class and the complex identities of race and gender in chapter 4. As African American historian Karen E. Fields and sociologist Barbara J. Fields have pointed out, "Inequality never stands merely as a fact, as the way things are or the way things are done: it requires moral reinforcement in collective beliefs."[13] Maintaining class differentials requires certain beliefs, as we shall see, including beliefs about identities such as race and gender and a confusion of privilege and power that will be addressed in the next chapter.

Class, Relationship, and Religion

If definitions of class in terms of stratification, including the categories of status, education, and income, are insufficient, what are the alternatives? Some established traditions define class in terms of the relationship between classes, linked to fundamental relationships that take shape at work.[14] While these traditions are often pushed aside because they seem to be inspired by the thought of Karl Marx, it is not at all necessary to subscribe to Marxian philosophy to appreciate them. The simple fact that most people spend the bulk of their waking hours at work points to the significance of the labor relationship, which

---

13   Karen E. Fields and Barbara J. Fields, *Racecraft: The Soul of Inequality in American Life* (New York: Verso, 2012), 277.

14   In the words of Michael Zweig, "Economics and Liberation Theology," in *Religion and Economic Justice*, ed. Michael Zweig (Philadelphia: Temple University Press, 1991), 34, "Class is a relational category, including all people who share some important aspect of relationship with another class of people. Production is a central aspect of human society and a key (but not simple) determinant of class."

is therefore not merely another relationship among others but has implications for all other relationships, public and private. In addition, neoliberal capital has managed to bond the working majority even deeper to its designs through the obligations of debt and borrowing, thus extending the realities of the labor relationship beyond work itself.[15]

The labor relationship is significant not only because this is where so many hours of people's lives are spent but also because this is where other existential matters are negotiated, connected to what might be considered the concerns of religion. As Filipino theologian Karl Villarmea has pointed out, using the example of the Philippines, the "basic feature and operation" of established labor relationships "correspond to the idea of sovereignty of God in classical theology."[16] For this reason, Villarmea argues that theologians need to question this relationship like they interrogate images of the dominant God.[17] One problem that makes our analysis more difficult is that these relationships are often internalized. Michael Hardt and Antonio Negri have used the term *biopower* to describe this internalization, arguing that "power can achieve an effective command over the entire life of the

---

15   In classical capitalism, this was also achieved through the company town and the company store. For the implications of debt on class relationships, see Filipe Maia, *Trading Futures: Toward a Theological Critique of Financialized Capitalism* (Durham, NC: Duke University Press, 2022).

16   Karl James E. Villarmea, "Transcendence in the Time of Neoliberalism: A Theological Reflection on the Employer-Employee Relationship and the Theological Struggle for Everyday Life," in *Faith, Class, and Labor: Intersectional Approaches in a Global Context*, ed. Jin Young Choi and Joerg Rieger (Eugene, OR: Pickwick, 2020), 236. Villarmea talks specifically about the labor relationship as established in Filipino law, but his thoughts apply to regulated labor relationships elsewhere as well. He also notes that in the Philippines, not to be part of the labor relationship is even worse, as there is no protection at all.

17   Villarmea, 254–55.

population only when it becomes an integral, vital function that every individual embraces and reactivates of his or her own accord."[18] Internalized biopower also touches on the concerns of theology and religion.

The grand claim of this chapter is that the increasingly unequal distribution of power at work for the sake of profit extraction profoundly shapes all of life in the twenty-first century, both human and nonhuman. The reason why the study of class is so crucial for the study of theology and religion is that class relationships bleed over into other relationships, making them highly relevant for noneconomic fields of study. Class relations have important implications for people's political agency, personal and communal relationships, relationships in religious communities, and even how theology, religion, and the world of ideas shape up.[19]

Relationships of class and labor are also where various other identities are being negotiated and shaped. Due to the existential character of work, the injuries of sexism and racism at work go deep. Moreover, perceived differences along the lines of gender and race carry weight because they make it possible for those who determine labor relationships to divide and conquer using gender and race and to maintain power. In this context, dealing with difference by admitting

---

18 Michael Hardt and Antonio Negri, *Empire* (Cambridge, MA: Harvard University Press, 2000), 24.

19 This is one of the key insights of the so-called new working-class studies: "Working-class culture does not exist only in the workplace, and . . . class conflict is not limited to the 'traditional' working class. This leads to questions about how class works in both communal and individual experience, how people make sense of their class position, and how consciousness of class might lead to collective action." Russo and Linkon, "New Working Class Studies," 10.

a limited number of women and minorities into the executive class does not remedy these problems but merely covers them up without fundamentally altering them. For all these reasons, the study of theology and religion can benefit from picking up questions of work, labor, and class in addition to the more commonly discussed questions of identity. Increasing numbers of investigations of "lived religion"[20] will benefit, as will recent theological conversations about "the everyday" (*lo cotidiano*[21]), which have yet to address matters of labor and class at the deeper levels.

While further study is needed on how class shapes politics, culture, identity, and religion, it is the topic of theology that interests us here. Given the fundamental importance of labor relationships in people's lives, it makes sense to consider labor as a matter of what Paul Tillich has famously called the "ultimate concern," even though this was not in his or any of his followers' purview. In Tillich's words, the ultimate concern defines what lies at the core of theology: "Our ultimate concern is that which determines our being or not-being. Only those statements are theological which deal with their object in so far as it can become a matter of being or not-being for us."[22] While Tillich was thinking about the concerns of existential philosophy, like questions of anxiety and meaning,[23] which are often still seen as the

---

20 For a recent overview of the study of lived religion since the late 1990s, see Kim Knibbe and Helena Kupari, "Theorizing Lived Religion: Introduction," *Journal of Contemporary Religion* 35, no. 2 (July 13, 2020): 157–76.

21 Ada María Isasi-Díaz, "Lo Cotidiano: A Key Element of Mujerista Theology," *Journal of Hispanic/Latino Theology* 10, no. 1 (August 2002): 5–17.

22 Paul Tillich, *Systematic Theology*, vol. 1 (Chicago: University of Chicago Press, 1951), 14.

23 Tillich, 49.

central topics of theological reflection, an analysis of class introduces concerns that may seem less deep and perhaps even mundane at first sight. To many theologians, conversations about labor and class appear to be irrelevant, as the topics are virtually absent in the literature.[24] Some well-meaning theologians draw problematic distinctions between the problems of hunger and poverty, which seem to be of a lower order, and the more genuine problems of theology, arguing that people need to be fed before they can engage in the questions of theology.

Theologian Terra Schwerin Rowe gets closer to the problem when she notes that "there is no more important task before humanity in the twenty-first century than to rethink models of relationship and exchange among humans and between humans and other-than-human matter." Religion is important, she notes, because it provides resources to envision "different modes of relational exchange, and articulate a compelling vision of what redemptive, sustaining, and life-giving—indeed, grace-filled—relations look like."[25] Yet even this proposal does not quite consider labor relationships and the concomitant power differentials, relinquishing an important part of the investigation into what alternative relationships and exchange would look like.

Consider the deeper significance of labor and class: there would be no being at all without reproductive and productive labor—in fact, without it there would only be not-being, to use Tillich's language. Reproductive labor, which

---

24   Exceptions include Rieger and Henkel-Rieger, *Unified*.

25   Terra Schwerin Rowe, *Toward a Better Worldliness: Ecology, Economy, and the Protestant Tradition* (Minneapolis: Fortress, 2017), xxxix.

in capitalist societies is mostly relegated to women and minorities—often with little or no remuneration because the economic system classifies it as "externalities"—is the precondition for everything, including productive labor. This is also the place for addressing the reproductive labor of the nonhuman world (see chapters 1 and 2), without which nothing would exist and without which the survival of living organisms would be impossible. In other words, labor relations appear to have a profound significance to life as a whole, which the study of theology has almost completely missed.[26] Based on these considerations, it might be argued that labor amounts to what nineteenth-century theologian Friedrich Schleiermacher has identified as a matter of "absolute dependence," the feeling of which he saw as the core of religion.[27] Schleiermacher's point that humans, while dependent on many things, are only absolutely dependent on the divine might be applied to reproductive labor in particular: there is no denying or escaping humanity's absolute dependence on it. In the aftermath of Covid-19, the notion of "essential labor" might approach a similar depth if taken seriously, as the world (and employers) may be more dependent on working people than anyone realized. All this to say that labor—and reproductive labor, in particular—must be

---

26 When labor has been the subject of theological reflection, it is often without much of an account of the tensions of labor relations. Miroslav Volf, *Work in the Spirit: Toward a Theology of Work* (Eugene, OR: Wipf & Stock, 2001); Matthew Kaemingk and Cory B. Willson, *Work and Worship: Reconnecting Our Labor and Liturgy* (Grand Rapids, MI: Baker Academic, 2020).

27 For the famous concept of "feeling of absolute dependence," see Friedrich Schleiermacher, *The Christian Faith*, ed. H. R. Mackintosh and J. S. Stewart (Edinburgh: T&T Clark, 1986), 12.

considered a fundamental term in the study of theology and religion.

Three important caveats are in order. First, defining class in terms of labor relations (reproductive and productive) is not about reducing the conversation to common stereotypes of the working class, like white men in blue overalls working in factories. On the contrary, the working class is the most diverse of all classes, a fact that is increasingly realized not only in the United States but even in Europe and many other places.[28] Neither does an emphasis on labor need to promote ableism. People with disabilities, the long-term unemployed, children, and the elderly also belong in this conversation because the inequalities and disparities of power at work that follow the motto "winner takes all" affect everyone and everything, even those whose relations to labor shape up differently. Even the one-third of the global population who are self-employed belong in this conversation about labor and the working class, as they are often street vendors or casual laborers for whom work is a matter of survival or small businesses where the owners work alongside the employees.[29] As pointed out in previous chapters, exploitative and extractive economies affect both people and nonhuman nature at every level, no matter their varying abilities.

---

28 "Class today is more feminine, migrant, multi-colored, with the most varied sexual orientations and identity." Various forms of oppression are interwoven, argues Mario Candeias, "Eine Frage Der Klasse: Neue Klassenpolitik Als Verbindender Antagonismus," in *Klassentheorie: Vom Making und Remaking*, ed. Mario Candeias (Hamburg, Germany: Argument, 2021), 463 (translation mine).

29 See Therborn, "Agenda for Class Analysis," 101. Of these self-employed persons, 30–31 percent live outside the wealthier countries.

Second, labor is a primary place of intersectionality where race, class, and gender come together, and it should not be too quickly separated into human and nonhuman. One of the most significant bonds is that what exploits people also exploits the planet, as argued in the first half of this book. Religious ethicist Cynthia Moe-Lobeda is right that "climate change may be the most far-reaching manifestation of white privilege and class privilege yet to face humankind."[30] This insight requires a closer look and a distinction of privilege and power, to which we will return in the next chapter, requiring a closer look at the forces that exploit and extract as well.[31]

Finally, labor relations are never merely about exploitation, profit extraction, and power differentials, as these relations also mark the location where the 99 percent who have to work for a living can build real power. Even the most alienated kind of work provides a place where working people have some modicum of power and agency that can contribute to shifting the labor relationship and therefore all other relationships, including religious ones and relations with the divine. This power and agency can be amplified and organized—if only for the simple reason that the economy depends on working people, no matter the level of automation or the pretenses of financial capitalism about its

---

30 Cynthia Moe-Lobeda, "Climate Change as Race Debt, Cass Debt, and Climate Colonialism," in Hughes, Martin, and Padilla, *Ecological Solidarities*, 61.

31 Unfortunately, Moe-Lobeda assumes that all "United States citizens who are white and economically privileged" (66) are the problem, adding that "people fitting this description of economic privilege occupy a wide-ranging economic strata" (79n22). This argument doles out equal blame to all but the poorest Americans, letting the elites off the hook and foregoing the solidarity of the 99 percent.

ability to run on its own steam. Already in the early days of capitalism, Adam Smith perceived that "the workman may be as necessary to his master as his master is to him."[32] The pernicious motto of the Indian Wars in the United States can hardly ever be applied to working people. Even in their wildest fantasies, no executive can ever claim that "only a dead worker is a good worker."[33]

Those who have to work for a living—99 percent of humanity—are, therefore, not as expendable as the dominant system wants everyone to assume. To be more specific, nothing can be produced, reproduced, built, or serviced without those whom we now call essential workers. And capitalism even needs the unemployed to keep the pressure on for those who are employed. The otherwise very useful critiques of work by antiwork theory, which have recently been picked up by some theologians, can sometimes appear as if they are forgetting the power inherent in work, even when it is alienated. And while the critique of alienated work under the conditions of capitalism is necessary, the question is how to reclaim the potential of work for producing and reproducing the flourishing of life. As antiwork theorist Kathy Weeks has concluded, "Life is part of work and work is part of life."[34]

---

32 Adam Smith, *Inquiry into the Nature and Causes of the Wealth of Nations*, ed. with an intro. and notes by Andrew Skinner (New York: Penguin, 1999), book 1, chap. 8. Smith notes, however, the power differential and that in situations of disagreement, employers can hold out much longer than workers due to their resources.

33 Erik Olin Wright, "Foundations of a Neo-Marxist Class Analysis," in *Approaches to Class Analysis*, ed. Erik Olin Wright (Cambridge: Cambridge University Press, 2007), 24, notes that "the exploiters actively need the exploited."

34 Kathy Weeks, *The Problem with Work: Feminism, Marxism, Antiwork Politics, and Postwork Imaginaries* (Durham, NC: Duke University Press, 2011), 232. Work is indeed part of life.

Class and Labor Relations

Among the topics that may seem too mundane for scholars of religion and theology to consider is that labor relations determine income. Yet when whole families end up on the street for lack of income and when entire communities are affected, income becomes an existential matter. In the United States, a larger share of people between the ages of eighteen and sixty-five live in poverty than in any other of the thirty-eight countries belonging to the Organization for Economic Cooperation and Development (OECD).[35] Labor relations are also linked to the fact that one-third of Americans live below the poverty line, as the majority below the poverty line are working hard and often hold down more than one job. At present, 26.5 percent of American families with children are *food insecure*, which means they do not have enough to eat even though they go to work every day. Labor relations are the cause that forces many people to live at the limits of existence even when there are no emergencies (like visits to the hospital, financial catastrophes, layoffs, or unplanned bills), a problem that also affects increasing numbers of those who consider themselves middle class but have reason to worry about the futures of their loved ones (children, parents, relatives), if not their own futures. The

---

Children enrolled in Montessori education, for instance, are proud to do what they call work. Telling them they were merely playing would be an insult to them and make them not feel taken seriously. For additional reflections on work and the limits of work, see Rieger and Henkel-Rieger, *Unified*, 9–32.

35 "Inequality—Poverty Rate—OECD Data," Organization for Economic Co-operation and Development (OECD), accessed March 25, 2022, https://data.oecd.org/inequality/poverty-rate.htm.

existential significance of labor relations is manifest also in the reduced life expectancy of working people.[36]

Labor relations determine class relations. Economists have estimated that approximately two-thirds of the working population in the United States can be considered working class, defined as having little or no power over their work and having little agency at work.[37] This lack of power not only is significant at work but has implications for a democratic society where agency and participation are seen as core values in political life and in the community. That many working people are not even asking for more power at work shows that the discrepancy between economic and political democracy still needs to be addressed. The lack of power at work is perhaps most visible in temp work in the United States, which is on the rise and is used to further weaken the power of regular work. The lack of regulation of temp work is an indicator of the lack of power of temp workers: the United States scores 0.3 for the second-to-last place (tied with Malaysia) on an OECD scale that goes up to 5 for regulations, with Brazil scoring 4.1, Thailand scoring 3.7, and Norway scoring 3.4. The fallout of this situation for all other workers is exemplified by the fact that firing them is easiest in the United States, which ranked last out of seventy-one

---

36 David Leonhardt and Stuart A. Thompson, "How Working-Class Life Is Killing Americans, in Charts," *New York Times*, March 6, 2020, https://www.nytimes.com/interactive/2020/03/06/opinion/working-class-death-rate.html.

37 According to Michael Zweig, 63 percent of Americans are working class, 35 percent are middle class, and only 2 percent belong to the capitalist class. Michael Zweig, *The Working Class Majority: America's Best Kept Secret*, 2nd ed. (Ithaca, NY: Cornell University Press, 2012), 36.

nations with a score of 0.5 (while Indonesia scored 4.1, Portugal scored 3, and Denmark scored 2.1).[38]

At the other end of the class spectrum is the class that determines labor relationships. Its power is manifest at the most basic level in its increasing wealth. The Covid-19 pandemic has made the connections more visible: America's billionaires added 2.1 trillion dollars to their portfolios by October 2021[39] during the exact same time period when millions of Americans lost their jobs—disproportionally affecting women, who globally had lost $800 billion in income by April 2021.[40] During that same time, so-called essential workers felt increased pressure to perform with little or no economic gain—an interesting example of the breakdown of the capitalist logic that increased demand translates into increased gain. Gaining from this labor, of course, are the companies and their stockholders, which shows that labor relations continue to matter more than many people realize. While some seem to think that economic gain in finance capitalism is a victimless zero-sum game—some theologians engage it at face value—it can hardly be considered an accident that American corporations, including universities and even churches, are pushing back hard against the efforts of

---

38 Matthew Desmond, "American Capitalism Is Brutal. You Can Trace That to the Plantation," *New York Times*, August 14, 2019, https://www.nytimes.com/interactive/2019/08/14/magazine/slavery-capitalism.html.

39 Juliana Kaplan and Andy Kiersz, "American Billionaires Added $2.1 Trillion to Their Fortunes during the Pandemic," Business Insider, October 18, 2021, https://www.businessinsider.com/american-billionaires-add-21-trillion-to-fortunes-during-pandemic-2021-10.

40 Courtney Connley, "In 1 Year, Women Globally Lost $800 Billion in Income Due to Covid-19, New Report Finds," *CNBC*, April 30, 2021, https://www.cnbc.com/2021/04/30/women-globally-lost-800-billion-dollars-in-income-due-to-covid-19.html.

their workers to organize at a time when their profit margins are growing.[41]

For good reasons, the Brookings Institution has called the economic fallout of the Covid-19 pandemic the most unequal recession in modern US history,[42] and the consequences of this rising inequality will be with us for many years to come. This serves as another example of what, during the Great Recession, I called the "logic of downturn,"[43] arguing that the full extent of the problem can only be seen by those who are experiencing the realities of downturn in their own bodies. To be sure, government support for working people in 2020 and 2021 was greater than in 2007–9, especially after the election of Joe Biden as president, but such support is easier to offer when corporations are not clamoring as hard for support, and it contributes very little to reduce inequality or transform fundamental labor relationships. While religious communities have sought to help those considered "less fortunate," they rarely understand the fundamentals of class relationships and how to support working people, who make up the majority of their own ranks.[44]

---

41 The Amazon corporation is, of course, the leading example of such pushback, but union busting is also increasingly common in major universities, including institutions of the Roman Catholic Church, whose social teachings have tended to support labor. Clayton Sinyai, "Mission-Driven Union Busting," Commonweal Magazine, September 17, 2012, https://www.commonwealmagazine.org/mission-driven-union-busting.

42 Zia Qureshi, "Tackling the Inequality Pandemic: Is There a Cure?," Brookings Institution, November 17, 2020, https://www.brookings.edu/research/tackling-the-inequality-pandemic-is-there-a-cure/.

43 Rieger, *No Rising Tide*. While the losses were socialized, the gains were privatized and funneled to the top.

44 Exceptions include religious support for the PRO Act before Congress, the work of the Interreligious Network for Worker Solidarity (IN4WS; https://in4ws.org/), and Clergy and Laity United for Economic Justice (CLUE; https://www.cluejustice.org/).

If class is examined as relationship, the question of money cannot be separated from the question of power. According to economist Michael Zweig, class can be defined as the "power and authority people have at work."[45] In essence, labor relationships in capitalist economies are between a small executive class at the top, which is in charge because it controls (even if it does not always directly own) the means of production and distribution, and a working class made up of the majority of the population (including a disproportional number of women and minorities), whose labor produces a surplus for those on the top. As the late David Graeber (an anthropologist) and David Wengrow (an archeologist) have argued, "Ruling classes are simply those who have organized society in such a way that they can extract the lion's share of . . . surplus for themselves."[46] Economist Richard Wolff sharpens the focus on class, noting that the concept of class "refers to the production and distribution of the surplus products of labor," adding that class is not necessarily more important than other factors but that it needs to be studied because it has been generally repressed from consciousness.[47]

By contrast, one widely celebrated example that shows a complete lack of class analysis is that of some religious communities writing thank-you notes to essential workers and handing out $10 gift cards to show their appreciation; "Essential Workers Feted with Encouraging Words, Gifts," North Texas Conference of the United Methodist Church, July 6, 2020, https://ntcumc.org/news/essential-workers-feted-with-encouraging -words-gifts.

45 Zweig, *Working Class Majority*, 3.

46 David Graeber and David Wengrow, *The Dawn of Everything: A New History of Humanity* (New York: Farrar, Straus and Giroux, 2021), 128.

47 Richard D. Wolff, "Religion and Class," in Rieger, *Religion, Theology, and Class*, 29, 30. This definition is distinct from older and simpler definitions of class as property/wealth

While power differentials are built into the labor relationship from the beginning, it is often overlooked that these differentials are quite substantial and appear to be increasing again. Although some political and even social relationships may have become more democratic—voting rights have been extended and women's rights expanded (despite seemingly never-ending pushbacks)—labor relationships have become less and less democratic. This development is key to understanding class, and it is the reason for reclaiming an understanding of class that some might reject as simplistic or outdated. Today, class and labor relationships look increasingly like they did in the early days of crude industrial capitalism rather than in the days of the capitalism shaped by the New Deal in the United States or during the height of the social market economies in Europe in the 1970s and 1980s. The paradox, as Graeber and Wengrow have observed, is that people who proudly insist on their political freedoms simply take it for granted that the economy has to be arranged in "strict chains of command."[48] Any sense of the complexities of class, which will become clearer in the next chapter and which are linked to the ecological challenges discussed in the two previous chapters of this book, will need to be developed with this in mind.

While the economy has been increasingly deregulated at the top—this is one of the markers of neoliberal capitalism—labor relationships have been increasingly regulated and constricted. As a result, working people have

---

or power/authority. Wolff notes that these insights correspond with Karl Marx's own interpretation of class.

48 Graeber and Wengrow, *Dawn of Everything*, 133.

lost not only income and benefits but also power, and it has become more and more difficult for working people to organize unions and make their interests count.[49] This is true especially in the United States, which has often used its influence to push for more restrictive labor relations in other countries as well. Even in Europe, where unions traditionally have had more power and where representatives of labor unions have enjoyed dedicated seats on the boards of corporations for decades, corporations have managed to extend their power over working people.[50]

As the executive class, the proverbial one percent, tends to remain out of sight in the everyday operations of neoliberal capitalism (despite certain individuals like Jeff Bezos and Elon Musk being highly visible), various management functions are taken over by those in the so-called middle class. Yet those in the middle are never quite in control of the labor relationship and, equally important, they have no choice but to work for a living as well.[51] According to some estimates, this middle class, defined as those who have some power over their work and some agency, makes up about a third of

49 Gordon Lafer and Lola Loustaunau, "Fear at Work: An Inside Account of How Employers Threaten, Intimidate, and Harass Workers to Stop Them from Exercising Their Right to Collective Bargaining," Economic Policy Institute, July 23, 2020, https://www.epi.org/publication/fear-at-work-how-employers-scare-workers-out-of-unionizing/.

50 Claus Schnabel, "Trade Unions in Europe: Dinosaurs on the Verge of Extinction?," VoxEU, Centre for Economic Policy Research, November 18, 2013, https://voxeu.org/article/trade-unions-europe.

51 The middle class finds itself in the space between these two classes (including professionals, small businesspeople, etc.), yet this class (to quote Karl Marx) "rests with all their weight upon the working basis" and at the same time increases "the social security and power of the upper ten thousand." Karl Marx, *Capital: A Critique of Political Economy*, trans. David Fernbach, 3rd ed., vol. 3 (London: Penguin Classics, 1981), chap. 17, section B 1d.

the population.[52] This class includes various levels of middle management, smaller business owners, and a vast array of professionals who have traditionally enjoyed some independence in terms of their labor relations. From certain vantage points, this middle sector can appear to have more affinity with the upper rather than the lower class, as it has some power, and—if classes are assumed to be linked to merit—its professional accomplishments might be seen as the basis for its success and promises for upward mobility.

However, the gap between the middle and the top should not be underestimated. In simple economic terms, the difference between millions and billions of dollars is quite significant,[53] as are the related differentials of power as well as the existential implications. Not having to worry about retirement, work, housing, or travels; being able to exert control over one's workforce; and often getting desired responses from politicians or governments are all existential matters. By contrast, in the current economic situation, most middle-class jobs tend to afford less power and influence than they used to: smaller business owners often work alongside their workers (and many small businesses are failing),[54] middle

---

52 Zweig, *Working Class Majority*, 36.

53 One million dollars in pennies stacked on top of each other would make a tower nearly a mile high; one billion dollars would make a tower almost 870 miles high, leaving the atmosphere of the earth. "Answers in Animation: What Is the Difference between Millions, Billions, and Trillions?," Truth in Accounting, August 7, 2019, https://www.youtube.com/watch?v=Om3FmWtf2AY.

54 Small business closures are not uncommon; about six hundred thousand businesses are closing every year. During the first year of the Covid-19 pandemic, two hundred thousand additional small businesses closed. Ruth Simon, "Covid-19's Toll on U.S. Business? 200,000 Extra Closures in Pandemic's First Year," *Wall Street Journal*, April 16, 2021, https://www.wsj.com/articles/covid-19s-toll-on-u-s-business-200-000-extra-closures-in-pandemics-first-year-11618580619.

managers have to follow the directives of their corporations (even CEOs are judged according to their performance for stockholders, although they often have golden parachutes), well-paid corporate lawyers receive their marching orders from management, professors are subjected to ever more detailed outcome evaluations, doctors' hands are increasingly tied by the insurance industry, and even big steeple pastors are expected to cater to ever more demanding donors and congregations. Even the one percent of the population who belong to the executive or ruling class are still topped by a 0.1 percent whose share of wealth (and power) had already tripled over that of the one percent by 2012.[55]

In this climate, even most business owners might want to reconsider their class alliances, as the US Department of Commerce figures show that in 2005, only 0.08 percent of all companies in the United States could be considered large corporations, employing 44 percent of all business employees.[56] While class can be defined by power at work, there are substantial differences between local bicycle store owners and corporate CEOs, for instance. And even though, unlike most small business owners, medium business owners might not work alongside their workers, they tend to share common adversaries, as challenges to their interests and

---

55 Howard R. Gold, "Never Mind the 1 Percent. Let's Talk about the 0.01 Percent," Chicago Booth Review, 2017, https://review.chicagobooth.edu/economics/2017/article/never-mind-1-percent-lets-talk-about-001-percent. The share of wealth of the 0.01 percent quintupled in the same time period.

56 See the account in Zweig, *Working Class Majority*, 15. The development over time can be seen in comparison with the first edition of this book: Michael Zweig, *The Working Class Majority: America's Best Kept Secret*, 1st ed. (Ithaca, NY: ILR, 2000), 17, reporting that in 1995, big business made up 0.07 percent of all businesses in the country, employing 20 percent of all business employees.

threats to their existence derive not primarily from their workers but from bigger companies and investors who have made it their business to put them out of business.

In any case, if class is considered in terms of relationships of power, it becomes clear that, as economist Michael Zweig notes, problems "arise not because some people are rich but because private profit and the power of capital are the highest priorities in the economic system."[57] Determined by legal precedent, the capitalist economy is dedicated to the profit of the stockholders alone, which has been the sole criterion for success for over one hundred years.[58] Although in more recent times, arguments have been made to take into account the benefit of "stakeholders" such as customers as well, the benefit of workers is still not part of the equation.[59] All in all, profit for elite groups continues to determine labor relations. How far labor has been pushed back in these relations may be exemplified by the iPhone X, which has a profit margin of 60 percent for Apple and its shareholders compared to 37 percent of component cost and 2.5 percent labor cost.[60]

In sum, class analysis needs to move away from never-ending conversations about the stratification of wealth—which is where classroom discussions and even academic

---

57 Zweig, *Working Class Majority*, 2nd ed., 74.

58 The precedent for this was established in 1919 in the case of *Dodge v. Ford Motor Company*, although there is some disagreement about how significant the legal aspect is in this case. What can hardly be disputed, however, is that it continues to be the accepted and expected way to do business in the United States.

59 Dennis Jaffe, "From Shareholder Primacy to Stakeholder Primacy: How Family Businesses Lead the Way," *Forbes*, March 16, 2021, https://www.forbes.com/sites/dennisjaffe/2021/02/24/from-shareholder-primacy-to-stakeholder-primacy-how-family-businesses-lead-the-way/?sh=4e8984fa21ed.

60 Therborn, "Agenda for Class Analysis," 104.

conversations on class often end up—and embrace an understanding of class in terms of labor relationships, where ever more extreme profits and power differentials are produced and reproduced. To be sure, thinking in terms of class as relationship also means that we are dealing not with individual interests but with classes that are never self-made—not even the executive class, despite its aura—but constructed in relation to all the other classes. This also means that blaming or demonizing individual members of the executive class or singling out individual members of the working class for acclaim demonstrates a fundamental misunderstanding of the topic of class.

Reconstructing Common Assumptions about Class

The problematic aspects of nonrelational understandings of class are now becoming clearer. Stratification theories presuppose that classes exist somehow like the layers of a cake that can be distinguished clearly, are mostly independent of one another, and can therefore also be studied in and of themselves. Questions of power are methodologically excluded from such definitions, which mirrors the prevalent methodological exclusion of the study of power in theology and religious studies.[61] Even the growing interest in inequality studies, which in some cases are beginning to replace stratification theories, is insufficient if labor relations are not considered. And critiques of capitalism that focus on

---

61 For a critique of the study of religion and theology along these lines, see Talal Asad, *Genealogies of Religion: Discipline and Reasons of Power in Christianity and Islam* (Baltimore: Johns Hopkins University Press, 1993).

property or wealth rather than class relationships overlook the fact that property needs to be understood and defined in terms of the relation of people who own property to other people who do not rather than merely in terms of the relation of people to the things they own.[62]

The problematic term *classism* demonstrates this lack of the study of relationship and power in its own way. The term suggests that the problem of class has to do with class stereotypes rather than with relationships of extraction or exploitation. As a result, the use of the term *classism* tends to imply that the problem can be overcome by doing away with class stereotypes, neglecting relationships of power and exploitation.[63] This is often how class is addressed in religious communities, which seek to "celebrate diversity" and consider their mission accomplished when millionaires and homeless people share the same pews.[64] Another problematic term that betrays an insufficient understanding of class is *consumerism*. Typical uses of the term tend to blame average consumers for consuming too much, ignoring and

---

62 See also Wright, "Neo-Marxist Class Analysis," 10.

63 This is not to say that an awareness of stereotypes and how they are produced does not have merit, but it is misleading to think that stereotypes themselves constitute class exploitation. For an example of this misunderstanding, see James N. Poling, *Understanding Male Violence: Pastoral Care Issues* (St. Louis: Chalice, 2003), 116–17, who assumes that a seminary professor represents the social class that is a source of the oppression of a factory worker: "It was in contrast to men like me that he was judged inadequate and expendable in society." While the power at work of professors might have been greater than that of factory workers, professors should perhaps not assume the innate value of their positions, realize that their salaries may not be much higher than those of factory workers, and develop a sense of who actually reaps the profits from the labor of factory workers. This might go a long way toward deconstructing stereotypes.

64 In a more sophisticated fashion, but along the same lines, religious sociologist Tex Sample has tried to create understanding and sympathy for "hard working people" in the church. Sample, *Hard Living People*.

thereby covering up the capitalist engines that drive consumption (see also chapter 1). Whatever solutions to over-consumption are suggested here lack deeper engagements of power differentials and asymmetrical class relationships.

Examples of nonrelational academic studies of class that neglect the question of power and relationship between classes abound. In religious studies, for instance, blue-collar religion is typically investigated without consideration of how it shapes up in relation to the executive class, even though this is a vital aspect of working-class existence.[65] Many authors still equate class with college degrees, assuming that everyone without a college degree is working class by default and anyone with a college degree is not.[66] Yet even a PhD degree does not necessarily lift people out of the working class, as academics should know, as more and more of them work as adjunct professors in truly dismal working conditions, where they earn less than the janitors at their school and with less job security and benefits. Moreover, classes other than the working class are rarely studied. The middle class appears to be taken for granted as normal, which seems to require little investigation. The executive or ruling class disappears from academic study not only because it may be

---

65 Sean McCloud, *Divine Hierarchies: Class in American Religion and Religious Studies* (Chapel Hill: University of North Carolina Press, 2007), explicitly rejects "deprivation theories" of class without letting on that there might be other ways of discussing class as relationship.

66 Even Williams, *White Working Class*, 43, operates with this definition, suggesting that "educational levels do not just reflect social class, they are *constitutive* of it" (emphasis in original). David Leonhardt, "College for the Masses," *New York Times*, April 24, 2015, https://www.nytimes.com/2015/04/26/upshot/college-for-the-masses.html. Forty-two percent of union members have at least a bachelor's degree; see Blado, Essrow, and Mishel, "Who Are Today's."

more difficult to get access to its operations (try to imagine what it would take to do an ethnography of the wealthy) but perhaps also because its ways of exercising power are typically out of sight and therefore out of mind.

While it is increasingly common to show some concern for poverty and poor people because there are so many—in both religious scholarship and religious communities—there is little concern for (if not outright resistance to) considering how poverty and the poor might be connected to wealth and the wealthy. The motto is always something like "fighting poverty" and never "fighting wealth." Theories of dependency, which gained prominence in Latin American liberation theologies and continue to shape the theological imagination, reclaim an analysis of power and relationship but often tend to feed into unhelpful generalizations, as if people in the Global North are unilaterally wealthy while all in the Global South are poor.

All of this changes if the study of class as relationships of power is introduced. The academic study of working-class religion, for instance—or of any other religious expression, whether it appears to be marked by class or not—must now take into account factors that are currently not being addressed. Likewise, religious communities' engagement of poor people must now consider the relationship between the "haves" and the "have-nots," going against the grain of a religious climate that typically locates the problem with the "have-nots" even when it seeks to help and provide "systemic" solutions.[67]

---

67 The solutions usually turn the burden back to the victims, including the encouragement to get more education and to develop their "assets" and advice for self-improvement in order to "level the playing field."

The same insights apply to the concerns of labor unions and worker centers for working people, many of which would benefit from deeper reflections on the fundamental character of the flow of power in labor relations. Too often, specific distortions, such as insufficient minimum wage laws or wage theft, are considered to be exceptions and moral aberrations rather than the rule.[68]

To be sure, substantial conversations about class as relationship present their own challenges, as this relationship is for the most part a conflictual one, deeply wrought by power differentials and marked by fault lines and struggles. Those who are bold enough to address such topics are quickly charged with committing grave errors and fallacies for which academics have developed their own terminology. Theologians who talk about class conflict are accused of embracing an "ontology of violence," as if conflict only comes into existence when it is mentioned.[69] In the social sciences, so-called conflict theories are often considered outdated, as they seem to replicate older theories developed by Karl Marx and others in the past. From the perspective of what has been called "deprivation theories," it seems to be

---

68 The problem of wage theft is rampant—more wages are stolen in the United States in any given year than thefts and robberies combined. See Brady Meixell and Ross Eisenbrey, "Wage Theft Is a Much Bigger Problem Than Other Forms of Theft—but Workers Remain Mostly Unprotected," Economic Policy Institute, September 18, 2014, https://www.epi.org/publication/wage-theft-bigger-problem-forms-theft-workers/. Wage theft is well suited for the mobilization of religious communities, since the moral problem is clear-cut. See the book by Kim Bobo, *Wage Theft in America* (New York: New Press, 2011). However, engaging wage theft exclusively often prevents religious communities from engaging the systematic distortions of labor relations.

69 John Milbank, *Theology and Social Theory: Beyond Secular Reason*, 2nd ed. (Malden, MA: Blackwell, 2006).

assumed that addressing class as relationship means talking about workers in negative terms, as deprived of or lacking things considered valuable by society.

The old accusation that those who address matters of class as relationship (and the concomitant power differentials) are instigating class struggle seemingly never dies. It stems from deficient definitions of class and power and finds a variety of expressions, like the following ones.

Widespread belief in individualism—whether by those who favor it or those who oppose it—is perhaps the most substantial hurdle for the discussion of class as relationship and of related class struggles. According to this belief, people exist in isolation from one another, create their own successes or failures, and are left to their own devices unless someone intervenes. Individualists celebrate what communitarians lament, but both assume that individualism is a fair description of reality. An understanding of class as relationship corrects this misunderstanding. It should not be hard to see that all people are connected in many ways, whether they know it or not. No individuals ever raised themselves, and all are constantly linked through economic interactions like labor relations, the production of goods and services, reproductive labor, and so on. Individualism is not a harmless conceptual misunderstanding but covers up relations of power and works in favor of those who benefit from the work of others. More specifically, individualism is the ideology of the executive elites who seek to cover up the fact that they are more connected than everyone else, as their power and wealth are produced by the many for the few. As a result, individualism covers up what should be called "class struggle from the top." Since the ruling class is usually more successful at this because it is better organized and has politics and law on its side (as already Adam Smith knew very well[70]), the working majority adopts this ideology to its detriment, and academic work that accepts the presuppositions of individualism, whether to support or critique it at face value, is flawed from the outset.

The assumption that class analysis does not apply to the United States because of class mobility is another factor that complicates the discussion of class. A prominent US feminist scholar of Buddhism once stated that she never considered class a significant matter of concern because class was the only matter she could always change about herself if she wanted to. The American Dream of making it from rags to riches is still widespread, although class mobility in the United States is lower than that of most developed countries, ranking behind Lithuania according to the 2020 World Economic Forum report.[71] And even if people intuitively know that they will not be able to improve their class position short of winning the lottery, they maintain the hope that their children and grandchildren will be more socially mobile. To varying degrees, this dream has also attached itself to the

---

70 "It is not, however, difficult to foresee which of the two parties must, upon all ordinary occasions, have the advantage in the dispute, and force the other into a compliance with their terms. The masters, being fewer in number, can combine much more easily; and the law, besides, authorizes, or at least does not prohibit their combinations, while it prohibits those of the workmen. We have no acts of parliament against combining to lower the price of work; but many against combining to raise it. In all such disputes the masters can hold out much longer"; Smith, *Inquiry*, book 1, chap. 8.

71 "The Global Social Mobility Report 2020: Equality, Opportunity and a New Economic Imperative," World Economic Forum, January 2020, https://www3.weforum.org/docs/Global_Social_Mobility_Report.pdf.

promises of various forms of what is currently called identity politics. As identity groups in the United States are rightfully struggling for liberation and empowerment, in many cases there is an unspoken assumption that their group might overcome the obstacles of class and reclaim the American Dream. Yet the fact that some women and racial and sexual minorities are assuming positions of leadership in the economy, politics, or religion does not mean that class relationships no longer matter or that oppression along the lines of gender and race is no longer relevant.

A major challenge to class analysis in the academy is that the label "Marxism" gets attached to any relational definition of class that includes reflections on the tensions between classes. Simply put, it is widely presupposed that the only reason why those who talk about class or class struggle do so is because they came across the topic in some of Karl Marx's writings—just like it is often assumed that people are rationalists because they read René Descartes, empiricists because they read David Hume, or idealists because they read a few of Plato's or Augustine's works. Yet while it seems inconceivable to many academics that anyone would be able to come up with an understanding of class (let alone class struggle) based on their own experience, this is exactly what happens to many working people when they take an honest look at their employment in the current economic climate. Common problems like wage depression, loss of benefits, or lack of power at work are part of the capitalist economy, determining the shape of labor relationships. This is not lost on many of those who experience these tensions in their own bodies, even if they have no idea of what Marx had to say about class.

In addition to the experience of class struggle in real time, reflecting on the relational character of classes is not new, as Greek, Roman, and medieval philosophers were aware of tense class relations, as were the Hebrew prophets, even though Greek and Roman philosophers usually took the side of the ruling classes while the Hebrew prophets sided with working people. This is not to say that class in ancient times is identical to class under the conditions of capitalism—the point is that class needs to be analyzed as a relational matter in any time period with an eye toward power differentials. The eighteenth-century fathers of capitalism, like Adam Smith and David Ricardo, had their own sense of the conflictual relations of classes. Smith put the challenges of class under the conditions of early capitalism quite clearly: "What are the common wages of labour, depends everywhere upon the contract usually made between those two parties, whose interests are by no means the same. The workmen desire to get as much, the masters to give as little as possible. The former are disposed to combine in order to raise, the latter in order to lower the wages of labour."[72]

Moreover, despite many misinterpretations, a sense of class struggle does not need to imply determinism, as if class determined absolutely everything, nor does it imply exclusivism, as if class was the only thing that mattered. What

---

72 Smith, *Inquiry*, book 1, chap. 8. Both Smith and David Ricardo distinguished three classes based on their source of income through wages, profits, or rent of land; Ricardo added that the interests of these classes were not merely contradictory but irreconcilable. See Chris Lorenz, "Representations of Identity: Ethnicity, Race, Class, Gender and Religion; An Introduction to Conceptual History," in *The Contested Nation: Ethnicity, Class, Religion, and Gender in National Histories*, ed. Stefan Berger and Chris Lorenz (New York: Palgrave Macmillan, 2008), 47–48.

does matter, however, is the analysis of power as it flows through class relationships and the effects of this power.

Finally, and this is perhaps the most important hang-up for contemporary academic sensitivities, addressing questions of class in terms of power and class as relationship can seem to be touching on matters of normativity.[73] In the current academic climate, any semblance of normativity tends to be seen as a lack of academic rigor, especially in the often-fraught relationship between religious and theological studies. But dealing with relationships of class and power does not necessarily have to imply a full-fledged normative position, even though it challenges academic claims of neutrality and objectivity that have long been questioned but are still in force. A blunt example may help illustrate the problem. Investigating the power relations of guards and prisoners in a Nazi concentration camp does not require a complete normative apparatus, but it hardly allows for indifferent neutrality and cold objectivity. And no study of guards or prisoners would ever be complete without considering the relation of one to the other, especially when the differentials of power are severe. The same could be said for labor relationships in the current economic situation, where corporations are increasing their power and reach, and the working majority, including the nonhuman natural environment, is paying the price.

---

73 Adolph Reed, *Class Notes: Posing as Politics and Other Thoughts on the American Scene* (New York: New Press, 2001), xii, summarizes the fallout in this way: "Pursuit of respectability in mainstream academic disciplines required shelving the idea of class struggle as an orienting principle of inquiry and debate."

In sum, raising topics of power and class relationship should not be seen as foreign to matters of academic study, including the study of religion and theology. Not only the economy but also politics, culture, and religion are linked to realities of power and class, and matters of power and class are not primarily extra-academic moral, ethical, or ideological concerns, to be added to a long list of other grievances and disclaimers.

Reconfiguring the Study of Religion and Theology in Light of Class

What might be the implications of studying class for the study of religion and theology? We have already touched on labor as a matter of ultimate concern, and theological reflection would do well to engage the topic whether it ultimately agrees with this interpretation or not. But there are other implications more specifically geared to matters of method.

One of the most important developments in the study of religion and theology has to do with a growing awareness that religion does not exist in a separate realm. As a result, in both religious studies and theology, methods of study increasingly incorporate insights from cultural studies and the social sciences, including anthropology and sociology. In addition, a more materialist understanding of religion, tied to what is now called the *new materialism* (engaged in the previous chapter), has contributed to more holistic perspectives, particularly via ethnographical studies, discourses on "lived religion," and what generally have become known as "thick descriptions."[74] Studies of class as relationship—a topic that is often absent even in the conversations of new materialism—can help broaden and deepen these perspectives further.[75]

In theological studies in particular, concerns for the social location of academic work, as well as sustained analyses of relationships of power, grew out of the work of different theologies of liberation. The various approaches, which developed in the context of liberation movements of the 1960s and 1970s around the globe, nevertheless often found themselves in conflict due to different emphases. When different liberation theologies (Black, feminist, Latin American, white, and so on[76]) in the Americas first began to engage one another in the 1970s, there was little agreement about which relationships of power mattered most. Feminists focused on gender, African Americans focused on race, and Latin Americans focused on economic relations—often more on North-South dependencies than on class.[77] In hindsight, a clearer sense of the realities of class might have helped them investigate how in capitalist societies, race and gender shape up in relation to

---

74 The notion of "thick description" was coined by sociologist Clifford Geertz. Clifford Geertz, *The Interpretation of Cultures: Selected Essays* (New York: Basic Books, 1973), chap. 1.

75 For efforts to broaden the understanding of religion in relation to class, see Rieger, *Religion, Theology, and Class*; and some of the essays in Rieger and Waggoner, *Religious Experience*.

76 A white liberation theologist in the US South, Frederick Herzog, published the first article using the term *liberation theology* in the United States, unaware that Gustavo Gutiérrez had already used the term in Latin America and that James Cone would publish his book by that title a few months later. Cone was not aware of Gutiérrez's work either. See Frederick Herzog, "Theology of Liberation," *Continuum* 7, no. 4 (1970): 515–24; and James H. Cone, *A Black Theology of Liberation* (Maryknoll, NY: Orbis Books, 1970).

77 See the proceedings of the first official meeting in Detroit in 1975 in Sergio Torres and John Eagleson, eds., *Theology in the Americas* (Maryknoll, NY: Orbis Books, 1976).

economic underpinnings. What all these approaches shared in common, however, was that they began to think about religion and the divine in terms of analyses of power, exploring alternatives based on the observation that both religion and the divine are often conceived of in terms of dominant interests.

That its subject matters develop in the orbits of dominant power may be the most important insight in religious and theological studies. Ignoring the flows of power creates problems not only because the subject matters of religion and theology are shaped by power relations but also because power relations shape the work of the interpreters. This is what distinguishes liberation theologies from liberal and other theologies, and some of this is making its way into the study of religion as well, as the focus of investigation continues to shift from big religious ideas and generic definitions of religion to popular and embodied practices of religion.[78] One of the most important shifts in this context is the insight that studying class as relationship (as well as more commonly studied relationships of race, ethnicity, gender, or sexuality) is not a matter of special interests but an integral part of the study of religion and theology as a whole.

In the study of religion and theology, a sense of the importance of power also developed in encounters with French theory. Jacques Derrida, Michel Foucault, Jacques Lacan, Gilles Deleuze, Pierre Bourdieu, and many others have

---

78 Examples in religious studies include Tomoko Masuzawa, *The Invention of World Religions: Or, How European Universalism Was Preserved in the Language of Pluralism* (Chicago: University of Chicago Press, 2005); and in theology, Kwok Pui-lan, *Postcolonial Imagination and Feminist Theology* (Louisville, KY: Westminster John Knox, 2005).

become household names in religion and theology in the United States, broadening the study of power by investigating what Lacan called the symbolic order and what Foucault would call discourse. Many of the insights of these approaches have proved helpful, as they too led to more material and complex understandings of religion and theology by investigating the power of language and culture and what has sometimes been dismissed on the left as less significant matters of "superstructure." Unfortunately, however, in US receptions of French theory, labor relations that were never completely absent in European minds were ignored. Many American scholars mistakenly assumed that labor and class relationships were irrelevant because seminal scholars like Foucault appeared to deal with other kinds of relationships.[79] And while the work of Bourdieu is commonly referenced when the topic of class comes up, many American scholars presume he did away with an analysis of class as rooted in capitalist labor relationships.

Bourdieu does indeed complexify notions of class by complexifying notions of capital, distinguishing among financial, technological, commercial, social, cultural, and symbolic capital.[80] Like other French theorists, however, Bourdieu's work needs to be understood as a response to specific concerns

---

[79] For an account of the role of work in Foucault's thought and its increasing significance in his later work, see Thomas Corbin and J. P. Deranty, "Foucault on the Centrality of Work," OnWork Newsletter, November 2, 2020, https://onwork.substack.com/p/foucault-on-the-centrality-of-work.

[80] Pierre Bourdieu, *The Social Structures of the Economy*, trans. Chris Turner (Cambridge: Polity, 2016), 194–95. That material conditions and cultural representations work together in shaping class is at the heart of what little current work there is on religion and class. See, in particular, McCloud, *Divine Hierarchies*; and Sean McCloud and William A. Mirola, "Religion and Class in America: Culture, History, and Politics," in *Religion and*

for class in Europe, in stark contrast to the American context, where class is rarely part of the conversation. Reclaiming class allows us to retrieve Bourdieu's reflections, which are rooted in a critique of capitalism. In his own words, "Financial capital is the direct or indirect mastery . . . of financial resources, which are the main condition . . . for the accumulation and conservation of other kinds of capital."[81] Bourdieu's sense of the complexity of capital and class, and the Weberian modesty that goes with it, does not have to mean that all things are equal. Bourdieu's insight of the mastery of financial capital over other forms of capital can also be applied to the mastery of financial capital over the working majority and its cultural and religious expressions, an insight that is overlooked by most contemporary scholars of theology and religion who engage matters of the economy.[82]

In applying and complexifying class analysis in religious and theological studies, it might be worthwhile to consider something like the *economic unconscious*, mirroring what Fredric Jameson termed the *political unconscious*,[83] shaped by

---

Class in America: Culture, History, and Politics, ed. Sean McCloud and William A. Mirola, vol. 7 (Leiden, Netherlands: Brill, 2009), 1–25.

81 Bourdieu, *Social Structures*, 194. Bourdieu also notes that when individuals perceive one another in terms of their status, they misperceive the economic and cultural capital that undergirds this status. See Elliot B. Weininger, "Foundations of Pierre Bourdieu's Class Analysis," in Wright, *Approaches to Class Analysis*, 101. For an account of a neo-Weberian approach, see Richard Breen, "Foundations of a Neo-Weberian Class Analysis," in Wright, *Approaches to Class Analysis*, 31–50.

82 See, for instance, Devin Singh, *Divine Currency: The Theological Power of Money in the West* (Stanford, CA: Stanford University Press, 2018). An exception is Tanner, *New Spirit of Capitalism*. But she does not draw out the implications for class analysis. See also my forthcoming review of Tanner's book in *Markets and Morality*.

83 Fredric Jameson, *The Political Unconscious: Narrative as a Socially Symbolic Act* (Ithaca, NY: Cornell University Press, 1981).

Lacanian and Marxian traditions and taking a cue from Sigmund Freud, the father of psychoanalysis. In the Freudian traditions, the unconscious is shaped in relationships, links to that which is being repressed, and is powerfully at work under the surface. While Freud focused mostly on family relations, Lacan extended this analysis to broader social and political relations and specific historical moments (the so-called ego's era).[84] Some work on the economic unconscious has already been done by theologians like Ulrich Duchrow and his collaborators and Bruce Rogers-Vaughn.[85] What still needs to be analyzed in more detail, however, is how the unconscious is shaped in labor relations specifically, both in individuals and in the collective unconscious of collectives and communities.

Dealing with class as relationship includes accounts of conflict and confrontation, which pose new challenges for religious and theological studies. In the mid-1980s and early 1990s, economists William K. Tabb and Michael Zweig elaborated this challenge perhaps more clearly than religious studies and theology. In the words of Zweig, "Liberation theology can be distinguished from liberal theology in that the former recognizes class conflict as a primary characteristic of society and positions itself consciously as an ally of one class against the other; whereas liberal theology, which also seeks to ameliorate the conditions of capitalism

---

84   Jacques Lacan, "The Function and Field of Speech and Language in Psychoanalysis," in *Écrits: A Selection* (New York: W. W. Norton, 1977), 71.

85   Ulrich Duchrow, Reinhold Bianchi, René Krüger, and Vincenzo Petracca, *Solidarisch Mensch werden: Psychische und soziale Destruktion im Neoliberalismus* (Hamburg: VSA Verlag, 2006); Bruce Rogers-Vaughn, *Caring for Souls in a Neoliberal Age*, New Approaches to Religion and Power (New York: Palgrave Macmillan, 2017).

and sees the need for structural change, denies the class-conflictual nature of society and proposes instead a plan for social harmony among all classes."[86] Tabb wonders about the agenda of "progressive churches," noting "the antipathy to the concept of class struggle, the emphasis on reconciliation, the belief in the possibility of convincing the powerful to change their ways and become more sensitive to the needs of the poor."[87] Since many theologians and scholars of religion as well as various religious communities tend to have a hard time dealing with conflict and tension, methodological change will not come easily.

The way forward in the study of class and religion is further complicated because investigations of conflict are rivaled by other categories. One of the themes that cut across many contemporary theologies is an aversion to what has become known as "dualisms" and "binaries" in favor of an appreciation of more fluid notions of otherness and difference that are linked to various postmodern and postcolonial sensitivities. Similar sentiments can be found in religious studies as well.[88] Prime targets of this critique are the old spirit/matter dualisms of Neoplatonic or idealist Christianity, which are indeed problematic because they separate what belongs together and, as the previous chapters have noted, have a history of harming the nonhuman world.

---

86 Zweig, "Economics and Liberation Theology," 38.

87 William K. Tabb, "Churches in Struggle: Liberation Theologies and Social Change in North America," in *Churches in Struggle: Liberation Theologies and Social Change in North America*, ed. William K. Tabb (New York: Monthly Review, 1986), xvi–xvii.

88 In Latin American liberation theology, one of the examples is Boff, *Cry of the Earth.* For US examples, see various chapters in Catherine Keller, Michael Nausner, and Mayra Rivera, eds., *Postcolonial Theologies: Divinity and Empire* (St. Louis: Chalice, 2012).

Other problematic dualisms and binaries include stereotypes of masculine and feminine, narrow concepts of inside and outside, and so on. Nevertheless, not all dualisms and binaries are equally passé, and some are gaining increased relevance today, like the tensions that mark labor relations under the conditions of neoliberal capitalism.

Dualisms and binaries that can be exposed and critiqued as products of dominant imagination, like the dualism of spirit and matter or of the immanent and the transcendent, must not be confused with the material dualisms and binaries that shape life under the conditions of neoliberal capitalism. While a growing sense of the complexity of relationships is valuable and can inform class analysis—poststructuralist notions of power, Foucauldian distinctions between *puvoir* and *puissance*, and postcolonial notions of hybridity and ambivalence have indeed broadened our horizons[89]—class analysis in particular reminds us of the growing differentials of power and the related tensions that mark our time, demarcating active dualisms and binaries that shape our lives. If indeed the rich are getting richer, the poor are getting poorer, and a rising tide does not lift all boats,[90] it should not be surprising that new dualisms and binaries are emerging that cannot easily be dismissed as baseless constructs or figments of the imagination. The methodological task is to integrate a deeper understanding of this fundamental

---

89 I have employed some of these concepts in my own work. Ambivalence, for instance, is one of the key concepts in my book *Christ & Empire*.

90 Shawn Langlois, "Rich Get Richer? Here's the Math," MarketWatch, November 30, 2020, https://www.marketwatch.com/story/rich-get-richer-heres-the-math-11606755825, describes the structural inequality present even in investing. The investments available to the wealthy are not only more lucrative but also less risky.

tension with newly gained sensitivities for complexity and difference (more in the next chapter).

As we broaden and complexify the study of class without losing sight of labor relationships, another academic development is informative for the study of religion and theology. Subaltern studies, originally developed in India and Latin America, has helpfully broadened the context of academic investigation in situations where the focus was perhaps too narrowly limited to matters of economics and the working class. In India and Latin America, subaltern studies has incorporated additional aspects of oppression, including social status (distinguished from class), caste, age, and gender.[91] This broadening of horizons corresponds with current North Atlantic concerns for complexity. Unfortunately, when these sensitivities were imported into the study of religion and theology in the United States via postcolonial studies, the original awareness of class that was never totally abandoned in India and Latin America was neglected. While subaltern and related postcolonial and decolonial studies in India and Latin America broadened the scope of their investigations in conjunction with an awareness of class, in US versions of these approaches, class was rarely present to begin with and was never reclaimed.

Reclaiming the study of class in the United States now will allow us to benefit more fully from the insights of subaltern,

---

[91] For the Latin American perspective, see the discussion in John Beverley, *Subalternity and Representation: Arguments in Cultural Theory* (Durham, NC: Duke University Press, 2004), 26. For the Indian perspective, see Vinayak Chaturvedi, ed., *Mapping Subaltern Studies and the Postcolonial* (London: Verso, 2000).

postcolonial, and decolonial studies.[92] Subaltern studies in particular can contribute to a deeper and more complex understanding of class in the United States. Antonio Gramsci, who coined the term *subaltern* in the early twentieth century, understood subaltern classes as those classes who, unlike the working class of his time, lacked unity and did not possess much class consciousness.[93] In contrast to Gramsci's Italy, in the contemporary United States, even the working-class majority experiences the subaltern's fragmentation and lack of class consciousness.[94] Many in the middle class, like professionals, independent contractors, middle managers, and small businesspeople, now experience the fragmentation of the subaltern as well. The notion of the "precariat" adds another facet to class analysis, as it designates a new subaltern that consists of people who otherwise appear to have little in common: gig economy workers, adjunct professors, freelancers, and so on, whose existence tends to be precarious because they often find it difficult to make ends meet

---

92 In my own engagements of subaltern and postcolonial studies, I have argued consistently for the inclusion of the notion of class; see, for instance, Joerg Rieger, "Liberating God-Talk: Postcolonialism and the Challenge of the Margins," in Keller, Nausner, and Rivera, *Postcolonial Theologies*, 211–14.

93 See Gramsci, *Selections*, 52. Peasants made up a substantial part of the subaltern. Gramsci's investigation focused on "the objective formation of the subaltern social groups," "their active or passive affiliation to the dominant political formations," "the formations which the subaltern groups themselves produce," the "new formations which assert the autonomy of the subaltern groups, but within the old framework," and "those formations which assert the integral autonomy [of those groups]."

94 Such fragmentation now even affects those who once were proud of their working-class identity. Joe Bageant, *Deer Hunting with Jesus: Dispatches from America's Class War* (Carlton, Australia: Scribe, 2009), reports that when he returned to the working-class town where he grew up and joined the workforce three decades ago, he was shocked about how much had changed.

but who have rarely been able to develop class consciousness.[95] In this context, the Occupy Wall Street movement's emphasis on the 99 percent helped reclaim a rudimentary class consciousness by emphasizing a sense of connection among those who have to work for a living and who are benefiting less and less from labor relations in neoliberal capitalism. While the 99 percent does not constitute a coherent class, there is a growing potential for solidarity that respects difference, which is significant for the work of theological construction, to be explored in the next chapter.

In Marx's thought, in contrast to the contemporary situation, class formation tended to be a more straightforward matter, as capitalist labor relations were more straightforward as well. Marx defined class as a relation in which the working class is clearly distinguished from all other classes: "In so far as millions of families live under economic conditions of existence that separate their mode of life, their interest, and their culture from those of the other classes, and put them in hostile opposition to the latter, they form a class."[96] This objective condition (sometimes called "class in itself"), Marx argued, needed to be integrated into the consciousness of working people ("class for itself"): "The economic conditions . . . transformed the mass of the people into wage-workers. The domination of capital has created for this mass of people the common situation with common

---

95 For an engagement of the precariat and a hopeful assessment of the potential of what has often been rejected as *Lumpenproletariat*, see Jan Rehmann, "Poverty and Poor People's Agency in High-Tech Capitalism," in Rieger, *Religion, Theology, and Class*, 143–56. For the notion of the precariat, see Standing, *Precariat*.

96 Karl Marx, "Eighteenth Brumaire (Sect. VII)," in Bottomore, *Dictionary of Marxist Thought*, 75–76.

interests. Thus this mass is already a class, as opposed to capital, but not yet for itself. In the struggle, of which we have only noted some phases, this mass unites, and it is constituted as a class for itself."[97] In other words, class emerges as the working majority works out its relationship with the executive class, and it does not exist in a full-fledged sense without community and political organization. In these developments, religion and theology play a role as well, for good or for ill, either by contributing to the formation of the community of working people or by detracting from it. Often overlooked but perhaps more relevant than ever, especially in the United States, is that the executive class is also characterized by community and political organization, as well as the bonds of religion.[98]

Given the various fragmentations of the working majority today under the conditions of neoliberal capitalism, the notion of the working class needs to be broadened, and Gramsci's notion of the subaltern enables us to take a closer look at all those who—due to their varied experiences of exploitation—have a stake in the critique of the system but otherwise appear to be unorganized and fragmented and therefore seem to have little agency. Broadening the notion of "class in itself" in the present moment—including the growing numbers of striking teachers, Amazon warehouse workers, taxi drivers, gig workers, and increasingly even

---

97   Karl Marx, *The Poverty of Philosophy*, trans. H. Quelch (London: Twentieth Century, 1900), chap. 2, sec. 5, 158. Marx adds that "an oppressed class is the vital condition of every society based on the antagonism of classes" (159).

98   See, for instance, Jeff Sharlet, *The Family: The Secret Fundamentalism at the Heart of American Power* (New York: Harper Perennial, 2009).

academics and professionals—leads to a broadening of what might be envisioned as "class for itself." Community, political organization, and cultural and religious practices can now not only be studied with these dynamics in mind; the studies themselves—some to be done by scholars of religion and theology—can make constructive contributions to class formation.

Any study of class, religion, and theology in the United States today can benefit from developing these broader horizons, as it can develop a clearer sense of the tensions and conflicts at work between those who control much of what is going on not only in the economy but also in politics, culture, religion, and the universities on the one hand and the proverbial 99 percent on the other, whose power appears to be quite limited at first sight. Yet it is precisely those who seem to have less power in these relationships who embody alternative interests that point to a different future, replete with worthwhile alternative religious practices, experiences of the divine, and theological rationales. Scholars of religious studies and theology overlook this at their own peril, especially since they are never merely uninvolved observers but always already pulled into the struggle due to their own place in the web of labor relations, whether they realize it or not.

Conclusions

In an essay titled "The Salience of Class in Britain and America," the authors provide data showing that in the United States, class may play some role in the smaller details of economic life but is rarely brought to bear on the bigger context of politics, where it seems to make no difference.[99] White working people in particular, as is often observed with some perplexity, vote against their own interests in significant numbers. This appears to be true also when it comes to matters of religion: in the United States, religion often upholds the dominant status quo, and working people appear to practice religion frequently against their own interests. As much of religion is oblivious or unsupportive of working people, it is not surprising that working people who are members of labor unions rarely reveal their identity in their religious communities and rarely hold these communities accountable to the concerns of labor. This is important to keep in mind not only for the critical and analytical work of religious studies and theology but also for constructive work.

Zweig writes, "As with every important social institution, religion both helps to shape and is shaped by the larger society in which it operates."[100] This is the basic point of analyzing class in the study of religion and theology. The relationship between religion and dominant power needs to be accounted for, and this account can aid efforts to transform it. The good news is that while Christianity has been shaped by dominant powers from its very beginnings, these powers have never been able to take over completely, and neither has capitalism in any of its variations.[101] This basic

---

99   Joseph Gerteis and Mike Savage, "The Salience of Class in Britain and America: A Comparative Analysis," *British Journal of Sociology* 49, no. 2 (June 1998): 271.

100 Zweig, "Economics and Liberation Theology," 8.

101 This is the common thread of Rieger, *Christ & Empire*.

insight inspires another look at religion. Liberation theologies, whatever their shortcomings may be, exemplify the inability of the dominant powers to take over Christianity altogether insofar as they continue to remind Christians of their often-neglected location on the fault lines of race, ethnicity, gender, sexuality, and class. Class analysis reminds us that, contrary to what the dominant powers want us to believe, those who are exploited in these relationships have some agency and—equally important—that taken together, they are never in the minority.

If the contemporary aversion to dualisms and binaries, found in both the theological academy and liberal Christianity, is revisited in light of class relationships that are often conflictual and tense, new insights emerge. At a time when power differentials are growing, especially at work, those who fail to engage these differentials of power tend to end up supporting those who benefit from them by default. That not even the middle class can claim neutrality in matters of class is perhaps the most crucial insight both for those who study religion and theology and for those who practice religion in the United States today.[102] This also means that the study of relationships of power at work can no longer be considered optional for scholars of religion and theology because it has consequences for virtually every aspect of the study of religion and theology, including comparative studies, interreligious dialogue, the relation of religion and

---

102   The role of the middle deserves greater scrutiny. See Norman K. Gottwald, "Values and Economic Structures," in Zweig, *Religion and Economic Justice*, 65–67. See also Duchrow, Bianchi, Krüger, and Petracca, *Solidarisch Mensch werden*, 200–245. This is also one of the basic issues addressed in Rieger, *No Rising Tide*, chap. 2.

science, and the study of the relation of religion, economics, and politics. None of these areas are exempt from the flows of power manifest and produced in labor relationships (formal and informal, productive and reproductive) under the conditions of neoliberal capitalism.

Finally, awareness of class relationships adds depth to the widespread and growing sense that everything is political, which is at the heart of political theologies. This awareness of class relationships can also lead to a better understanding of where politics can—and cannot—make a difference. Awareness of class relationships, finally, deepens the understanding that no religion can be studied (or should be practiced) without investigating the flow of power and its consequences, for good or for ill.

4

The (Im)possibility of Deep Solidarity

Reclaiming Privilege, Power, and Identity

There is nothing more dangerous to the dominant status quo than solidarity. Yet solidarity appears to be almost impossible to conceive in progressive circles today. According to an often-repeated adage sometimes attributed to Che Guevara, "When the American Left is asked to form a firing squad, it gets into a circle."[1] Yet while unity and solidarity can seem elusive for what might broadly be considered the progressive American Left, on the other side of the spectrum, things look different. The American Right has worked hard to pull together and build united fronts, a development that raises valid concerns about certain forms of unity. How might unity and solidarity be reclaimed by the

---

1   Danny Goldberg, "The Circular Firing Squad Isn't Amusing Anymore: The Left Is Tearing Itself Apart," *Nation*, July 19, 2017, https://www.thenation.com/article/archive/the-circular-firing-squad-isnt-amusing-anymore/.

progressive Left in this context? And what might this mean for theology in the Capitalocene?

In this chapter, the term *progressive Left* is used in a broad sense. It incorporates the adjective *progressive*, which is increasingly used instead of *liberal* in contradistinction to *conservative*. In theological circles, *progressive* refers to a wide spectrum that includes more liberal as well as more radical positions. Talking about the Left sharpens the focus of *progressive* while still leaving things open ended and affording space for diversity. In theological categories, the difference between *progressive* and the *progressive Left* is reflected in the differences between liberal and liberation theologies, manifest in the differences between theologies whose goal is to validate diversity and promote inclusion (often in terms of the dominant system) and theologies whose goal it is to engage exploitation, extraction, domination, and oppression.[2]

When addressing the topic of solidarity, it is important to clarify from the outset how not to approach this topic. Solidarity does not have to mean uniformity, sameness, or marching in lockstep, as it frequently does on the right. Disagreements are not necessarily detrimental to solidarity, and neither do all disagreements amount to the proverbial firing squads. In other words, solidarity does not have to mean abandoning a profound appreciation for diversity, difference, and multiple identities, which distinguishes the solidarity of the progressive Left from the solidarity of the Right.

---

2 A somewhat related tension exists in African theologies between theologies of inculturation and theologies of liberation. See Emmanuel Martey, *African Theology: Inculturation or Liberation* (Maryknoll, NY: Orbis Books, 1993).

Two common responses to the "circular firing squads of the Left" can be ruled out from the beginning. First is the centrist response. Centrists often seek to solve the problem by finding the lowest common denominator or by assuming that the truth lies somewhere in the middle. In this case, whatever is not considered to be in the middle can be quickly dismissed. In many cases, especially in mainline churches and their theologies, centrists are especially concerned about anything that is perceived to be left of center, while they are more likely to give a pass to everything else. Of course, as the political spectrum keeps moving further to the right, not only in the United States but around the world, the middle keeps moving further to the right as well.

The second response that can be ruled out is dreams of a unilateral position on the left that are built on assimilation and the acceptance of seemingly universal categories and points of view. This happens, for instance, when a singular category of domination is essentialized and made to trump all other categories. One example of this problem is historian Touré Reed's observation that postwar liberal positions, including Democratic presidential administrations from Kennedy to Obama (as well as Hillary Clinton's run for the presidency), have been race reductionist rather than class reductionist because they eliminated economic empowerment of minorities from other forms of fighting structural racism.[3] Reductionism will not bring unity to progressives on the left, and it will do little for theology in the

---

3 Touré F. Reed, *Toward Freedom: The Case against Race Reductionism* (New York: Verso, 2020), 1–14. See also Briahna Joy Gray, "Beware the Race Reductionist," Intercept, August 26, 2018, https://theintercept.com/2018/08/26/beware-the-race-reductionist/.

Capitalocene, which is why, in this volume, ecology is put into conversation with a more sustained analysis of class and with close attention to the challenges of racism and sexism.

Historical Notes on Solidarity and the Christian Left in the United States

In the history of the United States, progress (including theological progress) never materialized without solidarity—a concept that goes deeper than contemporary notions of allyship because it emphasizes connectedness and mutuality.[4] The various liberation movements in US history—abolitionism, suffragism, civil rights, ecojustice, Occupy Wall Street, Black Lives Matter, labor, and various socialist efforts—cannot be conceived without some solidarity bringing together diverse constituents. Each of these movements reshaped US history in significant and often lasting ways, even though the origins are not always remembered and the results are frequently taken for granted. The labor movement may serve as an example: under its leadership, the eight-hour workday was won after decades of struggle, child labor was ended, protection for women at work was introduced, and pension plans and even health care plans were developed. What may come as a surprise is that, unlike today, in the late nineteenth and early twentieth centuries, many faith communities and even

---

4   Jodi Dean, *Comrade: An Essay on Political Belonging* (New York: Verso, 2019), 15–23, investigates some of the limitations of the notion of allyship that is in vogue in certain progressive circles, as it considers identities as given, limits interaction by asking the allies to educate themselves rather than be educated by those with whom they want to ally themselves, and considers the struggle as a possession to which only some have a right and not others.

some mainline churches were supportive of labor struggles, the Left was not yet as ostracized as it is in religious and labor circles today, and many efforts were interracial.[5]

Solidarity in these movements was never about uniformity but allowed for different expressions, including religious diversity. Unlike in Germany, for instance, where religion was so closely linked to the dominant status quo that working people often had little choice but to emancipate themselves from it, in the United States, religion was more diverse and allowed for a greater variety of expressions—reflected in a broader variety of theologies as well. If in Europe the critique of religion often meant the rejection of religion altogether, in the United States, the critique of religion could also have meant the rejection of dominant religion and the embrace of alternative religious expressions even within Christianity itself. Examples from Christianity include various Anabaptist developments that grew out of the left wing of the German Reformation that came into their own on the American continent, like Mennonites, "Free Methodists" in the United States, early Pentecostal developments, minority religious traditions such as the Black churches, Christian socialist traditions, and a range of radical and liberation theologies discussed throughout this book.[6]

---

5 See, for instance, Matthew Pehl, *The Making of Working-Class Religion* (Urbana: University of Illinois Press, 2016); and Christopher D. Cantwell, Heath W. Carter, and Janine Giordano Drake, eds., *The Pew and the Picket Line: Christianity and the American Working Class* (Urbana: University of Illinois Press, 2016).

6 For a good overview of Methodism and early Pentecostal developments along these lines, see Donald W. Dayton, "'Good News to the Poor': The Methodist Experience after Wesley," in *The Portion of the Poor: Good News to the Poor in the Wesleyan Tradition*, ed. M. Douglas Meeks (Nashville: Kingswood Books, 1995). For fresh insights into the

Examples of alternative religious expressions also include labor and community organizers on the left constructively engaging Christian traditions in ways that are mostly forgotten today. Religion and labor, in particular, were at the heart of powerful transformations, including the Knights of Labor, Black and white social gospel preachers, and the 1908 Social Creed of the Methodist Episcopal Church, adopted also by the Federal Council of Churches, which made radical demands for "equal rights and complete justice for all men in all stations of life," labor rights for women, and "the most equitable division of the products of industry that can ultimately be devised."[7] Such radial demands, especially in regard to labor relations, have been dropped in the more recent version of the United Methodist Social Creed.

In many of these developments, solidarity emerged not primarily on the basis of progressive ideas but because people realized their shared interests, came together, and organized. As utopian socialists in the nineteenth century established communities all over the United States based on progressive visions, these communities rarely lasted for long, while organized working people began to make history

---

complex history of Christian socialism, see Gary Dorrien, *American Democratic Socialism: History, Politics, Religion, and Theory* (New Haven, CT: Yale University Press, 2021).

7   See, for instance, John C. Cort, *Christian Socialism: An Informal History* (Maryknoll, NY: Orbis Books, 2020); Juan Floyd-Thomas, "Seeing Red in the Black Church: Marxist Thought and African American Christianity," *Journal of Race, Ethnicity, and Religion* 1, no. 12 (November 2012): 1–46; and Joerg Rieger, "Christian Socialism," in *Routledge International Handbook of Sociology and Christianity*, ed. Dennis Hiebert (Routledge, forthcoming). For the 1908 Social Creed, see "Our Social Creed," United Methodist Church, June 27, 2019, https://www.umc.org/en/content/our-social-creed. See also David Burns, *The Life and Death of the Radical Historical Jesus* (New York: Oxford University Press, 2013); and Gary Dorrien, *The New Abolition: W. E. B. Du Bois and the Black Social Gospel* (New Haven, CT: Yale University Press, 2015).

and changed the course of the country in many cases. These organizing efforts attracted the interest and support of people who are rarely named in the same breath, like Karl Marx and Abraham Lincoln. Neither Marx nor Lincoln had much interest in utopian socialism, but both understood, in their own ways, the primacy of labor over capital and the value of organized working people for all kinds of progressive causes. This is an insight worth reclaiming after the Covid-19 pandemic has made us aware that society cannot function for long without what is now rightfully called "essential workers," which is not necessarily the case for many of the arbiters of ideas and capital.

Despite their differences and the obvious limitations of their times and places, Marx and Lincoln were quite clear about the benefits of labor unions, envisioning solidarity in practical terms, focusing not only on class but also on race.[8] Both Marx and Lincoln celebrated and welcomed the fact that the emerging working class in the United States was multiracial. In an 1864 letter to Lincoln, Marx famously noted that "labor cannot emancipate itself in the white skin where in the black it is branded."[9] The historical record shows that Lincoln responded positively to Marx's letter.[10] In his seminal work *Das Kapital*, Marx notes the broader

---

8   John Nichols, *The S Word: A Short History of an American Tradition . . . Socialism* (New York: Verso, 2015), 64, 92.

9   That line is from an 1866 letter to François Lafargue and repeated in *Capital*, as translated in Karl Marx, *Karl Marx on America and the Civil War*, ed. and trans. Saul K. Padover (New York: McGraw Hill, 1972), 275; Marx, *Capital*, trans. Fernbach; and Marx, *Capital*, trans. Fowkes, 301.

10 Karl Marx, "Address of the International Working Men's Association to Abraham Lincoln, President of the United States of America," International Workingmen's Association 1864, November 7, 1865, https://www.marxists.org/archive/marx/iwma/

context before repeating and expanding on that famous sentence: "In the United States of America, every independent workers' movement was paralyzed as long as slavery disfigured part of the republic. Labor cannot emancipate itself in the white skin where in the black it is branded."[11] This is not to insinuate that Marx was able to resolve the problem, but he clearly identified one of the major challenges that are still with us.

There is a longer history of concern for the relation of race and class on the left, including the Christian Left, which is mostly forgotten today.[12] While the abolition of slavery and emancipation were matters of life and death for those enslaved, these developments also signaled a broader emancipation of working people everywhere, both national and international. As Frederick Douglass noted, "The slave is robbed by his master, of all his earnings above what is required for his physical necessities, and the white man is robbed by the slave system, because he is flung into competition with a class of laborers who work without wages."[13] Southern white workers not only did, in fact, earn less than Northern white workers but also made less than Northern

---

documents/1864/lincoln-letter.htm. The letter was written by Marx and signed by the central committee of the First International.

11   Karl Marx, *Capital*, trans. Fowkes, chap. 10, "The Working Day," sec. 7.

12   See, for instance, the work of Frederick Herzog. For an interpretation, see Joerg Rieger, "Engaging Whiteness (More) Constructively: Conversations with James Cone and Frederick Herzog on the Future of Race and Class in Theology," *Review and Expositor* 117, no. 1 (2020): 58–71.

13   Frederick Douglass, *My Bondage and My Freedom*, ed. William L. Andrews (Urbana: University of Illinois Press, 1987), 188.

Black workers.[14] All this led to efforts for intersectional organizing across the South, identifying and building solidarity
at the level of the working majority—a majority that has
always been diverse in terms of race and gender, then and
now. Some were inspired by the theology of the social gospel
and its specific embodiment in the South.[15]

Enslavement of African Americans in the United States
did a tremendous amount of damage and negatively affected
most of the population, keeping down not only the enslaved
themselves but the majority of working people, as well as
shaping theology to the core. It has been argued that the
consequences of slavery are still visible even today. According to a recent article by Matthew Desmond, capitalism in
the United States continues to be so harsh in its treatment
of working people because it developed in the context of
slavery. Slavery produced a hierarchy of labor with clear
demarcations of who was at the top and who was at the
bottom—with those in the middle put into the service of
those on the top without gaining similar benefits and often
worse off than the middle class in the North. Moreover, the
meticulous methods of control over slave labor in the South
prefigured the subsequent use of similar methods to control
industrial labor in the North.[16] In addition, the exploitation

---

14   Michael Reich, "The Economics of Racism," in *The Capitalist System: A Radical Analysis
of American Society*, ed. Richard C. Edwards, Michael Reich, and Thomas E. Weisskopf
(Englewood Cliffs, NJ: Prentice Hall, 1986), 316, 318.

15   Anthony P. Dunbar, *Against the Grain: Southern Radicals and Prophets, 1929–1959* (Charlottesville: University of Virginia Press, 1981). See also "History of Social Gospel Personalities at VDS," Wendland-Cook Program in Religion and Justice, accessed March 25,
2022, https://www.religionandjustice.org/social-gospel.

16   Desmond, "American Capitalism Is Brutal."

of slave labor for the production of cotton was mirrored in the exploitation of land for the same purpose. Contemporary neoliberal capitalism continues to combine the exploitation of work and extraction of natural resources along the lines of class and race, which is why intersectional responses are needed for transformation.

The history of the Christian Left has often been genuinely intersectional. In many instances, the concerns of gender, race, and class came together organically, though, of course, never completely without tension. To be sure, the history of the Christian Left in the United States is not predominantly the history of white American males, as is often suspected. Many of its agents include women, African Americans, Native Americans, immigrants from around the world, and other minorities. Female African American civil rights leaders deserve a special place in this history because they brought together the concerns of race, gender, class, and religion in their own ways. Their names include Nannie Helen Burroughs, Ella Baker, Fannie Lou Hamer, and later womanist theologians like Delores Williams and Katie Geneva Cannon.[17]

Hamer's legacy is especially instructive, as she came to understand the need for building collective power beyond political victories. Cofounder of the influential Mississippi Freedom Democratic Party, some political setbacks led

---

17 For Hamer's work, see Monica M. White, *Freedom Farmers: Agricultural Resistance and the Black Freedom Movement* (Chapel Hill: University of North Carolina Press, 2021), 65–87. For the work of the earliest womanist theologians, see Delores S. Williams, *Sisters in the Wilderness: The Challenge of Womanist God-Talk* (Maryknoll, NY: Orbis Books, 2013); and Katie G. Cannon, *Katie's Canon: Womanism and the Soul of the Black Community* (Minneapolis: Fortress, 2021).

Hamer to focus increasingly on the building of networks of economic independence as the foundation of democracy. The cooperative efforts of Hamer's Freedom Farm Cooperative in Mississippi in the 1970s, parts of which were run by women, still offer inspiration and serve as reminders that political democracy cannot be conceived without economic democracy—and the same might be said for religious democracy (see chapter 2).[18] In a 1964 speech, Hamer explains how faith in God makes a difference: "All we have to do is trust God and launch out into the deep. You can pray until you faint, but if you don't get up and try to do something, God is not going to put it in your lap."[19] In other words, even faith in God—and related images of God—makes sense only in the context of cooperative work and solidarity. The legacy of the Christian Left, as well as the forms of solidarity that were part of it, cannot be understood without the fundamental contributions of African American traditions.

For the most part, solidarity was always more than just an idea in the history of the Christian Left: it was embodied by all those who stood shoulder to shoulder in the fight for transformation. Without this solidarity, many of the battles would not have been won. As historian Touré Reed notes, "Righteousness was not the basis for the movements that opened

18 For an account of Hamer's cooperative efforts, see Gordon Nembhard, *Collective Courage*, 178–87.

19 Fannie Lou Hamer, "'We're on Our Way,' Speech before a Mass Meeting Held at the Negro Baptist School in Indianola, Mississippi," Voices of Democracy, September 1964, https://voicesofdemocracy.umd.edu/hamer-were-on-our-way-speech-text/. Hamer believed that "'what God has done for Meshach, Shadrach, and Abednego' . . . God has done the same thing for Fannie Lou Hamer, Annell Ponder, and Lawrence Guyot" (par. 20).

opportunities to black Americans. Emancipation and even Reconstruction were produced by a convergence of interests among disparate constituencies—African-Americans, abolitionists, business, small freeholders and northern laborers—united under the banner of free labor."[20] In Frederick Douglass's famous words, "Power concedes nothing without a demand."[21] Such demands need to take the form of a serious push, bringing together political, economic, and religious democracy, based on the agency of the working majority and nonhuman nature (see chapters 1 and 2). Those who think that a few courageous voices speaking truth to power are enough may find that at the end of the day, they may well have the truth, but those in power still have the power.[22]

Divide and Conquer and Unite and Conquer

The history of the Christian Left shows that solidarity has successfully changed the history of the United States, which renders it dangerous and challenging to the status quo. Even though progressives are often unaware of the power of solidarity, it does not go unnoticed by the powers that be, which is why they try to subvert it in any way they can. One way to subvert solidarity is by offering support to select minorities.

---

20 Reed, *Toward Freedom*, 121.

21 Frederick Douglass, "If There Is No Struggle There Is No Progress," Black Past, 1857, https://www.blackpast.org/african-american-history/1857-frederick-douglass-if-there-no-struggle-there-no-progress/.

22 A comment I first heard on one of economist Richard D. Wolff's radio shows a few years ago, arguing for the need for worker cooperatives in addressing the failures of capitalism.

From the dominant perspective, it is always preferable to accommodate some people than to have the whole system challenged. Celebrating the diversity of minorities presents far less of a challenge than the solidarity of a majority.

Various mechanisms are employed to defuse solidarity. Efforts that promote inclusion and hospitality, prime concerns of contemporary liberal and mainline Christianity and theology, can be used to deter solidarity with little effort. It is not hard for the dominant powers to be inclusive and hospitable when they own the house where hospitality is to be offered, they oversee the system in which minorities are to be included, and they function as gatekeepers. Middle-class professionalism is another time-honored example that inhibits solidarity, as professional privilege promises a safe place in the system even for some minorities, typically in exchange for not challenging it and not rocking the boat. What is often overlooked is that opportunities for entering the professional world are quite limited and that professional existence under the conditions of neoliberal capitalism often has more in common with the working class than with the executive class. This is why not only academics but also doctors and lawyers are increasingly beginning to organize into unions, sending shockwaves through their institutions and receiving pushback at every step of the way.

Another way to deal with the challenges of solidarity is to co-opt it for the status quo. The political Right, in close alignment with the Christian Right, has produced its own forms of solidarity, which are designed to diffuse struggles for liberation. The first example is the old divide-and-conquer method, which not only undermines the more challenging forms of solidarity on the progressive Left but also produces a solidarity on the right that feeds back into the dominant status quo. And while divide and conquer may have various targets, it is particularly useful in dividing those who make up the majority of the United States: the proverbial 99 percent who have to work for a living, discussed in the previous chapter.

By dividing white, Black, Indigenous, Asian, and Latinx workers (now commonly referred to as BIPOC) as well as male, female, and queer workers, the dominant system makes sure that it will never be challenged by a majority. And while minority politics has its own place and potential that should not be underestimated, it is generally much easier to control. Racism has proven to be particularly useful in dividing the working majority in addition to benefiting the dominant powers by allowing them to bestow privilege on some but not others. As one author has observed, for good reason, "racism remains the key division within the working class."[23] The history of anti-Black racism in the United States can be traced back to the earliest days of the settlement of the American continent in seventeenth-century Virginia, where, as some historians have argued, a specific form of US racism was incubated by white masters with the goal to break up the naturally emerging solidarity of white and Black sharecroppers who worked side by side in the fields. The masters also managed to use this racism to produce an insidious solidarity between white sharecroppers and white

---

23 Sharon Smith, "Race, Class, and 'Whiteness Theory,'" *International Socialist Review* 46 (March–April 2006), https://isreview.org/issues/46/whiteness/.

masters, according to which the limited privileges afforded to the white sharecroppers by the white masters would cover up the differences between them. This move also covered up the fact that white and Black masters always had less in common than white and Black sharecroppers.[24] None of this means that there is not also a sense in which racism has older roots and runs even deeper, as Cedric Robinson and others argue, but the importance of this specific aspect of racial formation in the context of the United States must not be ignored.[25]

Cultural and religious developments have often been managed in similar ways: in churches and religious communities, divide-and-conquer methods have been employed to divide male, female, and queer Christians not only in order to support the dominant powers but also in order to define and control the meaning of Christianity theologically and determine the boundaries of orthodoxy. What is presented as that which is believed, according to the ancient formula of Vincent of Lerins, "everywhere, always, and by all" (*ubique, semper, et ab omnibus*), may be the faith not of the majority of Christians but of a small group of power brokers who have an interest in defining images of the divine in ways that shore up minority rule. To be sure, these power brokers are rarely

---

24 Theodore W. Allen's *The Invention of the White Race: The Origin of Racial Oppression in Anglo-America* (London: Verso, 1997), has investigated the beginnings of this phenomenon as far back as seventeenth-century Virginia. See also Lerone Bennett, *Before the Mayflower* (New York: Penguin, 1982).

25 See Cedric J. Robinson, *Black Marxism: The Making of the Black Radical Tradition* (Chapel Hill: University of North Carolina Press, 2000); and the summary of Robinson's work in Robin D. G. Kelley, "What Did Cedric Robinson Mean by Racial Capitalism?," *Boston Review*, January 12, 2017, https://bostonreview.net/race/robin-d-g-kelley-what-did-cedric-robinson-mean-racial-capitalism.

the theologians themselves; many theologians, often without being aware of it, are quite adept at reproducing what helps them get recognition, supports their institutions, and pays their salaries and honoraria. Examples of dominant theological construction include many of the classical attributes of theism, such as unilateral omnipotence or images of a white, hypermasculine, or imperial Jesus. These images employ the mechanisms of racism and sexism—often in hidden ways—in order to keep the dangerous power of the majority, based on common class interests, in check.

There is another aspect of the divide-and-conquer strategy that is often overlooked. We might call it "unite and conquer," linked to the insidious solidarity that white masters in the Southern plantation economy were able to forge with white sharecroppers—a racial solidarity that is not as natural as it seems. Unite and conquer later became the foundation of the "Southern strategy" in the United States that has been powerfully employed in Southern politics since the 1960s and that former president Donald Trump and many others have used and continue to use with great success. Here, white supremacy and white racism are employed to unite whites of all classes in order to create a majority for the purpose of winning elections and maintaining the power of a white elite. While the goal of this approach is to conquer, what exactly is conquered here is often overlooked. As would be expected, white supremacy effectively conquers both racial and ethnic minorities in the United States. The histories of slavery, Jim Crow laws, and current efforts of minority voter suppression in some Red States speak for themselves.

But—and this is the well-kept secret of unite-and-conquer methods—white supremacy also conquers working- and even middle-class white people by misleading them to believe that they have more in common with their white superiors than with fellow BIPOC working- and middle-class people. And, not coincidentally, unite and conquer controls their theologies by reproducing images of a white God, a white church, and a white religion. This identification of white people with the ruling class over against BIPOC populations is deep-seated and strong. As one eye-opening investigation has shown, many white people would rather die without health care than support the extension of health care to all if it would include and benefit BIPOC.[26] This insight is key to answering the puzzling question of why so many white people are voting against their own interests. Note that this is a problem not only in political elections but also in economic relations and even in religious communities and the church. In churches, these attitudes can also be seen in the fact that the power of mostly white donors and power brokers tends to be supported by other white members—frequently against their own interests. As Asad Haider puts it, "As long as racial solidarity among whites is more powerful than class solidarity across races, both capitalism and whiteness will continue to exist."[27] Or, as Martin Luther King Jr. understood, white poverty will continue alongside Black poverty if the white poor allow themselves to be turned against the

---

26 See the report in Jonathan Michel Metzl, *Dying of Whiteness: How the Politics of Racial Resentment Is Killing America's Heartland* (New York: Basic Books, 2020).

27 Asad Haider, *Mistaken Identity: Mass Movements and Racial Ideology* (London: Verso, 2018), 51.

Black poor based on race.[28] Once this is understood, the question becomes what to do about it.

The specific solidarity of white supremacist unite and conquer does not need to benefit all white people equally—the point is merely to make them *believe* that it does. As a result, unite-and-conquer solidarity serves to subdue the majority of white people to the interests of the white elites. Like with divide and conquer, unite and conquer is directed specifically against the solidarity of the working majority, and the results have been disastrous. Unite and conquer has split not only the working majority but even churches and religious communities, whose faiths have been hijacked and hollowed out systematically by big money since it started to push back against the opposition that emerged after the Great Depression and in the New Deal of the 1930s[29] and who continue to be split by similar forces in the first decades of the 2000s (like most recently the United Methodist Church).[30] Theology in the Capitalocene can no longer ignore the roots of what are often misinterpreted as mere theological differences.

The inextricable connections of race and class in the United States that Karl Marx and Frederick Douglass observed were once again pointed out by W. E. B. Du Bois in the 1930s:

---

28 Michael K. Honey, *To the Promised Land: Martin Luther King and the Fight for Economic Justice* (New York: W. W. Norton, 2019), 163.

29 Kruse, *One Nation under God*.

30 One of the players in several of these splits has been the so-called Institute for Religion and Democracy, whose funding derives from the Scaife Foundations, the Bradley Foundation, the Olin Foundation, Howard and Roberta Ahmanson's Fieldstead & Company, and other conservative sources. Laurie Goodstein and David D. Kirkpatrick, "Conservative Group Amplifies Voice of Protestant Orthodoxy," *New York Times*, May 22, 2004, https://www.nytimes.com/2004/05/22/us/conservative-group-amplifies-voice -of-protestant-orthodoxy.html.

racism, he noted, meant not only that Black people could be enslaved and exploited but that wages for white people could be kept low as well.[31] Or, in the words of Berkeley sociologist and law scholar Ian Haney López, who studies race and racism, "Racism is *a class weapon*" that harms everyone but the white elites.[32] In addition to racism, nationalism is another example of the unite-and-conquer strategy that is often used to defuse the transnational solidarity of working people everywhere, and it is not surprising that racism and nationalism commonly go hand in hand.

This takes us back to the key problem of labor relations, discussed in the previous chapter. Recall that the problem of labor is not limited to wages, as money, power, and influence over cultural and religious expressions are always connected. This means that racism cannot be defeated without dealing with class, and class struggle cannot be ended without dealing with race. This insight is an apt response to the pernicious campaigns of the Right against critical race theory, which want to make people believe that calling out racism means blaming whites and that challenging racism would only be beneficial for Black people. The appropriate retort, according to Haney López, is that many whites also suffer because of racism and they, too, can gain from cross-racial solidarity. This message, Haney López and his team of researchers found, is also more appealing to Black people,

---

31 W. E. B. Du Bois, *Black Reconstruction in America: Toward a History of the Part Which Black Folk Played in the Attempt to Reconstruct Democracy in America, 1860–1880*, 1st ed. (New York: Free Press, 1965), 700.

32 Ian Haney López, *Merge Left: Fusing Race and Class, Winning Elections, and Saving America* (New York: New Press, 2019), 6.

as they stand to gain a sense that whites have their own interests in (and valid reasons for) working together with Black people.[33]

Lack of class consciousness, as it developed along with racism, is a major reason why so many people have fallen for unite-and-conquer and divide-and-conquer methods, and even the progressive Left—including progressive theology—has not always seen these problems as clearly as it might have. In this climate, the charge of "class exclusivism" that is often leveled against the progressive Left is especially odd. What African American studies scholar Keeanga-Yamahtta Taylor has claimed of socialists might also be said about the religious Left and progressive theology: "No serious socialist current in the last hundred years has ever demanded that Black or Latino/a workers put their struggles on the back burner while some other class struggle is waged first. This assumption rests on the mistaken idea that the working class is white and male, and therefore incapable of taking up issues of race, class, and gender. In fact, the American working class is female, immigrant, Black, white, Latino/a, and more. Immigrant issues, gender issues, and antiracism *are* working-class issues."[34] While there may be some exceptions to this claim, Taylor is certainly correct about intersectionality in real life, which is most vital at work, where all the structures that dominate and exploit people come together.

In any case, political commentator and consultant Briahna Joy Gray is right that in the current climate, the fear

---

33 Haney López, 188. This is what he calls the "race-class message."
34 Keeanga-Yamahtta Taylor, *From #Blacklivesmatter to Black Liberation* (Chicago: Haymarket Books, 2016), 216.

of class reductionism—the belief that oppression along the lines of race and gender does not matter or will take care of itself when economic equality is achieved—is overblown and often used to defeat concerns about economic equality.[35] In faith communities and the work of theologians, class reductionism is hardly promoted anywhere, and even labor unions, who have at times put economic fights over racial ones, are increasingly seeing the light. Not recognizing the connections between race and class poses a danger that political scientist Adolph Reed has expressed in strong language: "In such conditions, opportunists and wackos can deploy the language of distrust with the destructive effect of provocateurs."[36] Unfortunately, most people active in progressive movements on the left, including religious communities and higher education, will have some experience with what Reed is saying.

What may come as a surprise is that this message of race and class solidarity can be communicated successfully to the broader American public. Haney López and his team tested messaging in the run-up to the 2020 elections and concluded, "The Right's core narrative urges voters to fear and resent people of color, to distrust government, and to trust the marketplace. The Left can respond by urging people to join together across racial lines, to distrust greedy elites sowing division, and to demand that government work for everyone."[37] When presenting the messages of both the Right and the Left to US voters who see themselves as centrists, Haney

---

35 Gray, "Beware the Race Reductionist."

36 Reed, *Class Notes*, xxiii.

37 Haney López, *Merge Left*, 74.

López's team found the argument of the Left more convincing. This is encouraging, as it allows for building the kind of solidarity that is needed for transformation and as those ready to enter into solidarity include many ordinary people. Haney López expresses the hope that "many are likely to merge left if economic and racial issues are appropriately and comprehensively intertwined."[38]

Touré Reed puts it this way: "Treating race as if it exists in a world apart from class . . . deprives those of us who would like to live in a more egalitarian society the ability to distinguish between committed ideologues—like Nazis and Klansmen—and reflexive racists who might be won over via platforms based on common interest."[39] Solidarity may be possible after all, but what else might it take, and what might all that imply for theology in the Capitalocene?

Distinguishing Privilege and Power in the Quest for Deep Solidarity

The fundamental problem of race and class is summarized succinctly by African American historian Barbara J. Fields, coauthor of the book *Racecraft*[40] with her sister Karen E. Fields, a sociologist. Discussing white supremacy, Fields notes, in agreement with historian C. Vann Woodward, "Not all white people have the same power and not all white

---

38 Haney López, 221.

39 Reed, *Toward Freedom*, 130.

40 Fields and Fields, *Racecraft*.

people are in the same class position."[41] Along the same lines, Keeanga-Yamahtta Taylor points out that "racism in the United States has never been just about abusing Black and Brown people just for the sake of doing so. It has always been a means by which the most powerful white men in the country have justified their rule, made their money, and kept the rest of us at bay."[42] Add to that writer Allan G. Johnson's observation that "every form of privilege has an economic dimension, which means that the nature of capitalism as a system profoundly affects how privilege and oppression work."[43]

Following these trains of thought, a distinction needs to be made between privilege and power, which will be instructive for the study of religion and theology as well. It should be fairly clear that under the conditions of white supremacist racism, all white people have privilege, whether they realize it or not. Racial privilege conveys many advantages in the dominant system; it can provide substantial benefits, and it is always systemic, which means that one can be privileged without feeling privileged. Add to that the fact that some

---

41 "Even if you can argue convincingly that they all have bigotry and prejudice—even if you do that—then you have to acknowledge that not everyone has the same level of power and responsibility." Barbara J. Fields, Karen E. Fields, and Daniel Denvir, "Beyond 'Race Relations,'" *Jacobin*, January 17, 2018, https://www.jacobinmag.com/2018/01/racecraft-racism-barbara-karen-fields.

42 Taylor, *#Blacklivesmatter to Black Liberation*, 216.

43 Allan G. Johnson, *Privilege, Power, and Difference*, 3rd ed. (New York: McGraw Hill Education, 2018), 35. Johnson's example is that of race, which in the United States developed in conjunction with capitalism (35–36). Johnson goes on to explain that the connections between capitalism and race can be both direct and indirect, including enslavement and the development of the notion of whiteness as well as the control of white workers (40–42).

forms of privilege are more deeply entrenched and therefore harder to notice and change.[44]

Nevertheless, systemic privilege does not always translate into power, which is also systemic. Despite the fact that all white people benefit in some ways from white racial privilege, they do not all have the same power—although some power usually goes with privilege. According to sociologist Max Weber, power is the ability of one person to exercise influence on another person against their interest. Extending that definition to social systems, the question becomes where the ability to influence others against their interests is located. Labor relations, discussed in the previous chapter, exemplify well what is at stake: white warehouse workers enjoy white privilege compared to BIPOC warehouse workers, but they do not have the same power—economic, political, or cultural—as white warehouse managers or white warehouse owners, let alone the seven billionaire heirs of Sam Walton, who control Walmart. This insight tends to come as a rude awakening to many white working people, but it is even more unsettling for white professionals, white academics, and white religious leaders who enjoy a great deal of white privilege and even some power but whose power to truly impact the system in significant ways is embarrassingly small. This insight also tends to come as a surprise to many nonwhite people, who—because they fail to distinguish between privilege and power—often overestimate what white people can actually do. The result is disappointment

---

44 See Johnson, 25, on the paradox that one can be privileged without feeling it. Johnson points out that diversity programs usually address the "milder forms" of privilege, reluctant to recognize the more entrenched forms (23).

and frustration all around. As a rule of thumb, it seems that too much focus on privilege covers up the question of power (and the related topic of class).

The confusion of privilege and power benefits the dominant system, as it hides the location of dominant power behind the notion of privilege and allows for assigning blame to those with some privilege but less power. In many cases, well-meaning people of faith who realize their privilege accept the blame, as well as the related charge to make a difference. Neglecting the distinction of privilege and power, members of the white middle class tend to assume that they can change the world with regard to at least racism and sexism and perhaps even some ecological destruction. Following the advice attributed to anthropologist Margaret Mead—"Never doubt that a small group of thoughtful committed individuals can change the world. In fact, it's the only thing that ever has"—they may even collaborate with a few of their friends and make efforts to become allies of some with less privilege. Yet Mead's adage not only overestimates the power of anyone not part of the executive class and leads to misplaced blame; it also fails to grasp the problem. In the end, the failure to distinguish privilege and power and to understand the lack of power amounts to yet another abortive rehash of the American Dream, this time for activists.

Unfortunately, middle-class Christians who are led to think that they can change the world because of their cumulative racial, gender, and sexual privilege still rarely pose much of a threat to systemic forms of domination and oppression, let alone to the system of neoliberal global capitalism. Confusing privilege, of which they may have a considerable amount, and power, of which they have much less, they are oblivious to the need for broad-based solidarity of those who are not running the system. Activism must change or it will become increasingly irrelevant.

So how can the progressive Left pull together and make a difference, and what might be the lessons for theology in the Capitalocene? Worrying about the political and religious Right unified by racism, sexism, and nationalism has helped create some cohesion. But this is not enough, not even when things take a turn for the worse, as happened during the years of the Trump presidency. Keeanga-Yamahtta Taylor takes us back to the relations of labor and class when she talks about a "*potential* for solidarity"[45] that has to do with the fact that "when one group of workers suffer oppression, it negatively affects all workers."[46] There is, according to Taylor, a "material foundation for solidarity and unity within the working class."[47] Adolph Reed talks about a politics that "presumes a concrete, material basis of solidarity—not gestures, guilt-tripping and idealist abstractions."[48] In other words, solidarity emerges in relation to the common pressures experienced by the working majority—without this material foundation, it may not be an option. This is something I have emphasized in my own work as well, coining the notion of *deep solidarity* in the context of the Occupy Wall Street movement,

---

45 Taylor, *#Blacklivesmatter to Black Liberation*, 208.

46 Taylor, 209.

47 Taylor, 215.

48 Reed, *Class Notes*, xxvii. He continues, "To the extent that differences are real and meaningful, the best way to negotiate them is from a foundation of shared purpose and *practical* solidarity based on a pragmatic understanding of the old principle that an injury to one is an injury to all" (xvii–xviii). See also 207–11.

where a rudimentary understanding of class emerged again in the United States after a long silence.[49] This brings us back to intersectional class analysis, which is based not on moral imperatives to well-meaning people (often demonizing the wealthy) but on a clear-sighted analysis of power in relation to privilege.

That there are material foundations for solidarity means that it is not primarily an ideological sleight of hand, as it often is for conservatives who promote a false sense of solidarity via racism, sexism, and nationalism; neither is solidarity a moral imperative for privileged people, as is often the case with liberals and some progressives. Unfortunately, these two options are all that most people imagine to be possible, even those who have studied the relations of privilege and power.[50] The true potential for solidarity, by contrast, is rooted in the realities of exploitation and oppression that affect the many, not just a few. This was one of the lasting insights of the Occupy Wall Street movement's recognition of the difference between the symbolic 99 percent majority and the one percent minority. Keeanga-Yamahtta Taylor helpfully pushes the boundaries of progressive politics on the left when she notes that the popular idea of white people becoming allies to Black people "doesn't quite capture the degree to

---

49 Rieger and Kwok, *Occupy Religion*; Joerg Rieger, "Occupy Wall Street and Everything Else: Lessons for the Study and Praxis of Religion," *Peace Studies Journal* 5, no. 1 (January 2012): 33–45, http://peacestudiesjournal.org/volume-5-issue-1-2012/. For a more extensive discussion of deep solidarity, see Rieger and Henkel-Rieger, *Unified*.

50 See Johnson, *Privilege, Power, and Difference*, 9. Johnson suggests a moral solution: "The trouble we are in cannot be solved unless people who have privilege feel obligated to make the problem of privilege *their* problem," proposing the need for action, beyond moral appeals (63–65; emphasis in original).

which Black and white workers are inextricably linked."[51] To be sure, this link exists whether people realize it or not, as it has to do with the structures of exploitation at work in the dominant system and not merely with personal experiences. In order to visualize these structures, a basic awareness of class is required.

Some theologians might find such a down-to-earth understanding of solidarity too common and mundane or perhaps even too self-absorbed. Yet self-interest does not have to be confused with selfishness. Even Jesus's commandment to love one's neighbor as oneself concedes self-interest, and self-interest becomes more relevant when it is understood that the interest of the neighbor and the interest of the self are linked. Martin Buber's and Emmanuel Levinas's interpretations of this commandment, which argue in their own ways that the neighbor is always part of the self, set the stage. Our analysis builds on these insights but clarifies the foundation of the relationship as grounded not in some metaphysical or ethical claim but in the common experience of exploitation, domination, and oppression.[52] Nevertheless, despite their differences, both Buber's and Levinas's arguments and my own construct solidarity not primarily as a moral demand but as rooted in a reality that can be observed. Solidarity is a fact of life that needs to be deepened and developed, not just an idea or a task.

---

51 Taylor, *#Blacklivesmatter to Black Liberation*, 215.

52 A sustained analysis of oppression and power is missing in their major works: Martin Buber, *I and Thou*, trans. Ronald Gregor Smith (New York: Scribner, 1986); and Levinas, *Totality and Infinity*.

Still, many theologians prefer metaphysical concepts like human dignity or moral notions of human rights. To be sure, such concepts can also contribute to the development of notions of solidarity, but the problem is who gets to define them. Current notions of human dignity and human rights are often shaped by dominant interests, downplaying definitions of dignity and rights that are more in tune with the needs of the 99 percent, such as the dignity of human labor and creativity and the right to be employed. Other concepts, like the "reverence for life" (the motto of humanitarian Albert Schweitzer, also a theologian), may be more helpful, as they point to what is indeed sorely lacking in the dominant neoliberal capitalist system: reverence and respect for all life.[53] Reverence for life has the additional advantage that it creates space not only for human life but also for non-human life and ecology more broadly. But even this concept might benefit from a clearer understanding of what it is that welds us together in real life across racial, gender, and national boundaries—namely, a fundamental lack of power in the capitalist system that affects the human 99 percent, all of nonhuman nature, and any theology that 99 percenters are doing.

More recently, activist Valerie Kaur has deployed the notion of deep solidarity without mentioning the origins and other uses of the term. She distinguishes it from what she calls "shallow solidarity" and states, "Shallow solidarity

---

[53] Albert Schweitzer, *Civilization and Ethics*, trans. John Naish (London: A & C Black, 1923), xvi: "Ethics is nothing else than reverence for life. Reverence for life affords me my fundamental principle of morality, namely that good consists in maintaining, assisting and enhancing life, and that to destroy, to harm or to hinder life is evil."

was based on the logic of exchange—*You show up for me, and I will show up for you.* But deep solidarity was rooted in recognition—*I show up for you, because I see you as part of me.* Your liberation is bound up in my own."[54] While mutuality is indeed an important element of solidarity, what is left open in Kaur's definition is the crucial question of how these various liberations are bound up with one another. Deep solidarity, as we are using the term, requires an analysis of capitalism, which is conspicuously absent in Kaur's references to the more easily refuted problems of state violence, bombing campaigns, and soldiers sent to war. By contrast, the analysis of capitalism is also central to Taylor's and Reed's arguments. Talking about deep solidarity in material rather than idealizing or moralizing terms addresses common problems in popular progressive narratives, which fail to distinguish privilege and power.

Having addressed an often-overlooked lack of power, we can now take another look at privilege. Many progressives are no doubt worried that solidarity talk can lead to erasing the differentials of privilege between BIPOC and white people and therefore to letting white people off the hook. Worse yet, certain ways to talk about solidarity might neglect profound Christian processes of confession of sin and repentance for white racial and gendered privilege, which are crucial to any theology in the Capitalocene.

To state it clearly, erasing the differences between BIPOC and white people—or between genders and sexualities—and

---

54 Valarie Kaur, *See No Stranger: A Memoir and Manifesto of Revolutionary Love* (London: Oneworld, 2020), 78.

letting people off the hook is not how solidarity is built. This is why deep solidarity is not promoting uniformity but actively embracing difference as a constructive element in the formation of solidarity, with special attention to the role that BIPOC and women are already playing and how it can be expanded (without, of course, imposing additional burdens on them). The role of white people in all of this—of those who enjoy white privilege (or heterosexual male privilege)—needs special scrutiny, which once again requires the distinction of privilege and power.

The mistaken assumption that privilege equals power creates several problems for solidarity and for dealing with privilege. It raises expectations on all sides for what white people can do to fix the problems of white privilege and white supremacy. As a result, privileged people typically overestimate what limited power they have, and others hope for outcomes that cannot be achieved if privilege does not equal power. Not surprisingly, frustration and failed efforts of transformation are common, augmented by a misdirected sense of sin and guilt. It is, therefore, not uncommon for well-meaning white people, especially in the middle class, to blame themselves either for not being able to change things or for being the primary cause of all exploitation and oppression. Likewise, it is not uncommon for BIPOC and women to assume that they are on their own, except perhaps for a few white or male allies who seek to divest themselves from power they do not have without developing whatever limited power they do have. As a result, the agency of such allies is quite small and doomed to failure. In response to these problems, the development of deep solidarity can help deal by distinguishing privilege and power with a clearer sense of how the differentials of privilege can be addressed more constructively in order to develop communal power. In the process, more appropriate understandings of sin, guilt, and repentance can develop, eliminating common attitudes of false humility among some or defensiveness among others.

If privilege and power are distinct, confession and repentance are meaningless without an understanding of how repenting for unchecked privilege can translate into embracing alternative forms of power that lead to combatting sin and guilt and working toward liberation. The prophet Isaiah, remembering the oppression of the Babylonian Empire of the sixth century BCE, has God say the following words: "Is such the fast that I choose, a day to humble oneself? Is it to bow down the head like a bulrush. . . . Will you call this a fast, a day acceptable to the Lord? Is not this the fast that I choose: to loose the bonds of injustice, to undo the thongs of the yoke, to let the oppressed go free, and to break every yoke?" (Isa 58:5–6). Inspired by this passage and armed with a distinction of privilege and power, confession and repentance for sin can be practiced—for instance, where white 99 percenters break the bonds of white privilege and white supremacy by siding with their BIPOC siblings against the dominant power represented by the executive class. In the process, privilege can be addressed, and the power of solidarity is set free. The reversal that is characteristic of repentance is also reflected in the Jesus movement, which is not afraid to introduce divisions where false peace rules ("Do you think that I have come to bring peace to the earth? No, I tell you, but rather division!"; Luke 12:51) in order to create alternative solidarities: "Whoever does the will of God is my brother and sister and mother" (Mark 3:35). The difference between the solidarity on the right (based on family and ideological identity) and on the left (based on common projects of liberation) could not be clearer.

Deep solidarity is not about letting privilege off the hook, and neither is it about claiming sameness and identity or becoming "color-blind." Needed for solidarity is not sameness or identity but merely an understanding of the fact that the few are benefiting at the expense of the many, which is how the neoliberal capitalist status quo maintains itself. As a result, this situation can only be changed by the many, not the few, which requires solidarity and not just allyship. In this context, the distinction of privilege and power does two things for the formation of solidarity: it enables the acknowledgment of white privilege, and it allows for the subversion of dominant power. On this basis, the limited power white privilege bestows on all white people can be put to use in transforming the dominant power to which unchecked white privilege contributes, thereby deconstructing white privilege itself.

The distinction of privilege and power benefits from an awareness of class and labor relations in the formation of solidarity. Barbara Fields helps us see things more clearly when she notes that "we're living in the midst of the most unrelenting and successful period of class warfare in American history. The targets are working people, all kinds of working people, and the more we allow ourselves to look away from structural political reasons for it, the more we are helping those who have their feet on our necks."[55] Without awareness of the tensions of class (as developed in chapter 3), solidarity remains elusive, and the capitalist exploitation of the 99 percent and extraction of the planet's resources will continue, supported by racism and sexism. Note that this affects not only politics and economics but also the practice of religion and the study of theology. In fact, faith communities and their theologians tend to make things worse when they seek to promote reconciliation without dealing with the root causes of the conflict.

Directing our attention to class in this context does not mean ignoring racial, ethnic, gender, and sexual difference— just the opposite. There is a common misunderstanding of which Barbara Fields reminds us: "When someone in the press says working class or working-class voters, they invariably mean white people. They forget that most Afro-Americans in this country are working people. Most Latinx people, however you define that ambiguous term, are working people. Southeast Asian migrants, most of them are working people, and indeed the same is true of a good many East Asian migrants."[56] The working majority is more diverse than any other social formation the world has ever seen, disproportionately BIPOC and female, and this is fundamental to solidarity as well as the work of theology in the Capitalocene.

---

55 "Even if you can argue convincingly that they all have bigotry and prejudice—even if you do that—then you have to acknowledge that not everyone has the same level of power and responsibility." Fields, Fields, and Denvir, "Beyond 'Race Relations.'"

56 Fields, Fields, and Denvir.

In sum, deep solidarity accomplishes two unexpected things: not only is it built on a challenge of privilege and genuine appreciation of difference, but it also manages to employ differences for the common good and the power of resistance. These differences can be multiple, tied simultaneously to race, ethnicity, gender, sexuality, nationality, and even religion. Deep solidarity, therefore, amounts to a reversal of anything the Right might call solidarity. As the solidarity of the Right is guided by sameness and by privileged racial and religious identities, the solidarity of the Left is guided by experiences of economic exploitation that affect the working majority, compounded by race, ethnicity, gender, sexuality, and nationality. Significant guidance comes, therefore, from those who experience these compounded forms of exploitation, domination, and oppression in their own bodies because they are more existentially affected by the system than anyone else. Deep solidarity needs to start from below, which does not mean that the burden of the work should be on the shoulders of the proverbial "least of these," but vision and leadership have roots where the pressures are greatest.

Theology is not an afterthought of solidarity but strikes at its roots. The solidarity of the Right offers a theological justification of the status quo, building on the perennial religion of empire that equates the divine with the dominant powers. This is why its solidarity implies everyone looking alike, talking alike, thinking alike—often misinterpreted by theologians as "orthodoxy"—along with nationalist white racial and heterosexual gender identity. The solidarity of the progressive Left, by contrast, finds the divine elsewhere, informed by the incarnation of Christ in solidarity with the multitude of common people everywhere rather than the elites. This insight requires the transformation of the status quo, building on the revolutionary religious expressions of Moses, the Hebrew prophets, Jesus, and even a surprisingly radical Paul, who writes about a God who "chose what is foolish in the world to shame the wise" and who "chose what is weak in the world to shame the strong" (1 Cor 1:27).[57] These multiple foundations of the faith account for another sort of orthodoxy that is grounded not in sameness but in what we might call theological solidarity, where orthodoxy and ortho-praxis are always connected and mutually shape and reshape each other.

As the deep solidarity of the progressive Left aims at the transformation of privilege and power, it also provides the tools for it. The transformation of privileged straight white men may serve as an example: if they reappropriate the limited power their heterosexual white privilege affords them to help build the power of the working multitude, vari-ous things change for good. Troubling one's alignment with the dominant powers and rejecting unite-and-conquer strat-egies (including false orthodoxies) will have consequences, as those who go down that route long enough will be marked as traitors who eventually cannot go home anymore. Con-version and repentance are built into this model, as the transformation of white heterosexual privilege is inevitable when deep solidarity is embraced and developed, although it will be a slow process that can last a lifetime. The holiness

---

57 For this radical Paul, see Rieger, *Christ & Empire*, chap. 1.

traditions of Christianity were aware of this and embodied it at their best—a development that some contemporary authors have reinterpreted as a refreshing form of theological queerness in relation to the straitjackets of the dominant system.[58]

Note, finally, that deep solidarity differs substantially from the approaches offered by communitarianism that appeal to many faith communities as well as scholars of religion and theology. While organic communitarian notions of community are more flexible and malleable than right-wing uniformity and can produce a certain solidarity, they are limited in their ability to deal with diversity. As a result, communitarian traditions have some trouble not only with inclusivity but also when those who are truly different become agents. Even when they seek to be inclusive and hospitable, communitarian models tend to remain self-referential, as inclusion happens on the terms set by the community. Communitarians might be able to tell their children that "others are people like us," which is a vast improvement over the Right's assumption that "others are lesser people than us." The deep solidarity model, by contrast, goes an important step further when it affirms that "we are like other people," which puts an end to the self-centeredness of the dominant system and opens up the possibility for mutual relationships that can take into account differentials of power. In our current economic moment, this would include the insight of the

58   For the queerness of the Wesleyan traditions, see Keegan Osinski, *Queering Wesley, Queering the Church* (Eugene, OR: Cascade Books, 2021). For the political connotations of the holiness traditions, see Joerg Rieger, *No Religion but Social Religion: Liberating Wesleyan Theology* (Nashville: Wesley's Foundery Books, 2018).

99 percent that "we are like essential workers everywhere," an international perspective that profoundly reshapes how many people who enjoy privilege in the current situation think of themselves, leading to the permanent reconstruction of dominant power.

Some Lessons of Class for the Politics of Race and Gender

Having established the importance of class, labor, economics, and ecology throughout this book, it is important to end with a few thoughts on what this might mean for ongoing reflections on gender and race and the kind of solidarity that might be possible, as everything is connected. For theologians, this touches on issues that have been at the heart of our work since the early days of various liberation theologies half a century ago. In what follows, the conversation will be limited to the notions of gender and race, picking up the time-honored triad of gender, race, and class as they have been presented in womanist theology and elsewhere. Keep in mind, however, that these concepts are always porous, and none of them is absolute (whether ontologically or biologically), which is to say that gender can be taken to include references to sexuality, race can include notions of ethnicity as well, and all of these categories might be considered "queer" in the broader sense of not conforming to any predetermined status quo.

The study of intersectionality, defined as "a way of understanding and analyzing the complexity of the world, in people, and in human experience,"[59] provides an initial framework for reflecting on the relations of gender, race, and class. Credit for the initial development of notions of intersectionality goes to African American women as well as Chicanas, Asian Americans, and Native women, where the pressures of race, class, and gender have long shaped collective experience. One of the foundational contributions to the subject is the work of the Combahee River Collective, a group of African American queer socialist feminists who introduced the matter of sexuality into the conversation of intersectionality in the 1970s.[60] In theology, the Mudflower Collective was among the pioneers.[61] In many of these early collaborations, capitalism is named as the context for various forms of domination and oppression.[62] Patricia Hill Collins, one of the leading theorists of intersectionality, has proposed a fundamental distinction between what she calls the matrix of difference and the matrix of domination, which are often at loggerheads.[63] Touré Reed helps us contextualize

---

59 Patricia Hill Collins and Sirma Bilge, *Intersectionality* (Cambridge: Polity, 1985), 25.

60 See the brief history in Hill Collins and Bilge, 63–87. The term *intersectionality* was coined by legal scholar Kimberlé Crenshaw in 1989 (81). For one proposal on how to use the term in theological studies, see Kim and Shaw, *Intersectional Theology*, which unfortunately does not touch on the notion of class in any substantial way.

61 The Mudflower Collective, *God's Fierce Whimsy: Christian Feminism and Theological Education* (New York: Pilgrim, 1985).

62 See, for instance, the "Third World Women's Alliance," launched by the Black Women's Alliance in New York City and the Puerto Rican women's movement in 1970. See Hill Collins and Bilge, *Intersectionality*, 75. The Mudflower Collective is perhaps not as clear, but they also note that "racial/ethnic oppression and sexism are constitutive elements of class dynamics in the United States." Mudflower Collective, *God's Fierce Whimsy*, 77.

63 Margaret L. Andersen and Patricia Hill Collins, "Why Race, Class, and Gender Still Matter," in *Race, Class, and Gender: An Anthology*, ed. Margaret L. Andersen and Patricia Hill Collins (Boston: Cengage Learning, 2010), 4–11.

this distinction when he identifies the juxtaposition of two related matrices—inclusion and acceptance of others versus economic equality—as the legacy and limitation of liberal politics.[64] This distinction is crucial for theology in the Capitalocene.

Concerns for gender and race are often discussed in terms of the matrix of difference, which argues for an increased appreciation for differences, acceptance, and inclusion into the system. Such efforts are prominent in religious communities and in seminaries and universities, which have been adding offices for "diversity, equity, and inclusion" across the board in recent years. We should add that when class appears at all in any of these settings, it is usually in terms of the matrix of difference as well. This creates confusion, as class exploitation is not something to be included, appreciated, accepted, or celebrated. Still, religious communities have tried this on occasion by inviting wealthy people and homeless people into the same building so that they can sit in the same pews. Such efforts overlook that the fundamental problem of class differentials is not "classism" (a term that pops up often when class is referenced in theological education), in the sense of class stereotypes that would need to be given up. If differentials between classes rest on relationships of exploitation and domination, the problem is not class stereotypes but class structures—which will need to be abolished rather than appreciated. Class, therefore, is a matter not of the matrix of difference but of the matrix of

---

64 Reed, *Toward Freedom*, 131.

domination, which addresses differentials of power and how to overcome them.

These insights have implications also for dealing with gender and race, as these categories might also be addressed more fruitfully in terms of the matrix of domination than the matrix of difference: Should women, racial and ethnic minorities, and queer people merely be included in an updated system, or is a more fundamental liberation necessary that would restructure the system altogether? This is not to say that appreciation for different identities tied to gender and race should be given up—and neither should we neglect identities tied to class and class consciousness. In Hill Collins's and Bilge's words, "Identity is central to building a collective we."[65] Even in the matrix of domination, identities are important as constructs that can function in various ways, for good and for ill, but they require closer scrutiny in terms of their formations, functions, and contributions to resisting and overcoming domination.

Critical theorist Nancy Fraser provides another model that sheds light on these topics when she discusses the fundamental differences between what she calls the struggle for recognition and the struggle for redistribution, two options that are often played off against each other. Fraser's observation, right after the fall of communism in the Soviet Union in the 1990s, that the struggle for recognition has risen to dominance is still valid thirty years later. The struggle for recognition is concerned with the recognition of various identities—racial, ethnic, gender, and sexual—by

---

65 Hill Collins and Bilge, *Intersectionality*, 135.

the dominant system, and it is antithetical to the struggle for redistribution. Fraser's succinct description of the situation in the academy is still on point, perhaps more so than twenty-five years ago: "Cultural domination supplants exploitation as the fundamental injustice. And cultural recognition displaces socioeconomic redistribution as the remedy for injustice and the goal of political struggle."[66] In other words, in the current situation, the focus on defending identities, ending cultural domination, and winning recognition dominates over the focus on exploitation. The result, as Fraser notes, is "a decoupling of cultural politics from social politics, and the relative eclipse of the latter by the former."[67] Fraser notes that these shifts are more pronounced in the United States, wondering, "Where else . . . does ethnicity so regularly eclipse class, nation, and party?"[68] arguing that this makes the politics of difference less internationally applicable.[69] While theologians might observe some of these shifts even in international church bodies such as the World Council of Churches, one wonders whether an unrecognized hegemony of US theological paradigms (many international theologians are trained in the United States) might be at work.

It is perhaps not surprising that these sentiments emerged just as capitalism declared its ultimate victory in the 1990s with the fall of Soviet-style communism. Yet thirty years

66 Nancy Fraser, "From Redistribution to Recognition? Dilemmas of Justice in a 'Post-Socialist' Age," *New Left Review* 212 (July 1, 1995): 68.

67 Nancy Fraser, *Justice Interruptus: Critical Reflections on the "Postsocialist" Condition* (London: Routledge, 1996), 2.

68 Fraser, 197.

69 Fraser, 200.

later, reclaiming a sense of what Fraser calls the struggle of redistribution would befit the situation, as capitalism is showing serious flaws and relations of class and exploitative labor relationships shape life everywhere in an ever more extreme fashion from top to bottom, exacerbated by extractive relationships with the nonhuman world.

Fraser proposes a constructive solution that brings together concerns for redistribution and concerns for recognition. While responses to recognition often tend to be at cross-purposes, she argues that responses to redistribution can bring the two struggles together. This happens when the concern for identity changes its focus, working toward transformation rather than merely toward recognition. To sharpen Fraser's point, we might add that efforts to gain recognition by the dominant system, exemplified by widespread models of hospitality and inclusion (two key efforts in contemporary theologies and faith communities), often work against the transformation of the dominant system.

Fraser's emphasis on the struggle for redistribution resonates with the global problem of growing exploitation and extraction that marks the Capitalocene, discussed throughout this volume. Nevertheless, based on the analysis of class presented in the previous chapter, the concern for distribution does not quite reach the core of the problems of neoliberal capitalism. The massive inequality of distribution itself has to be understood in terms of the inequalities of labor relationships. Unequal distribution of wealth and power is directly linked to the exploitation of working people and the planet. Talking about distribution without talking about production or reproduction is insufficient in terms of both the analysis of the problem and the solution, as fixing distribution without fixing relations of production and reproduction would not change the world for very long (even if it were miraculously accomplished somehow).

For theologians, this throws new light on the roles of religious communities and even the divine. Acts 2:42–47 and 4:32–37 are often quoted in reference to the politics of distribution and redistribution in early Christian communities, where, according to the texts, all shared their wealth and no one had need. In these conversations, production is often overlooked, although it is also part of these ancient Christian and Jewish traditions. The ministry of Jesus, for instance, is not merely about the distribution and sharing of wealth but also about the production of it. As some New Testament scholars have pointed out, Jesus seems to have organized the productive powers of the common people at a time of exploitation by large landowners and an imperial tax system that funneled wealth from the bottom to the top.[70]

The key argument that permeates all chapters of this book moves us forward in this debate as well: it is in the struggles linked to production and reproduction (human and nonhuman) that the struggles for recognition and distribution, as well as the matrices of difference and domination,

---

70 Although not a New Testament scholar, Karl Kautsky makes the interesting observation that early Christianity promoted "a communism in the distribution" of the "articles of consumption." When applied to agriculture (unlike in the cities), he argues that this communism could also lead to a "communism in production, in joint organized labor." See Karl Kautsky, *Foundations of Christianity: A Study in Christian Origins* (New York: New York International, 1925), 345. In recent New Testament studies, Richard A. Horsley's *Jesus and the Powers: Conflict, Covenant, and the Hope of the Poor* (Minneapolis: Fortress, 2011) has portrayed Jesus as an organizer.

come together. This throws new light on questions both of identity and of class. What if the most prominent concerns are no longer inclusion, acceptance, tolerance, or hospitality—relationships that may be formed along the way to liberation? What if the most prominent concern is productive and reproductive agency (human and nonhuman), as it directly pushes back against the exploitative and extractive relationships that dominate in a capitalist economy? What if the goal is not inclusion but systemic transformation? Transformation rests on the members of the working majority, which includes women and sexual, racial, and ethnic minorities, as well as nonhuman forces, becoming productive and reproductive agents in their own rights in ways that lead to the reshaping of systems of exploitation and domination. This challenges, from the outset, any solutions that amount merely to the revitalization of the fantasy of the American Dream for working people and minorities, and it challenges a kind of identity politics that only amounts to the inclusion into the status quo, covering up the systemic structures of power that keep exploiting working people, minorities, and all that is not human. By putting transformation over inclusion, the challenges of systemic racism, systemic sexism, and systemic ecocide can be addressed at deeper levels as well.

In the 1960s, Martin Luther King Jr. famously wondered, "What does it profit a man to be able to eat at an integrated lunch counter if he doesn't earn enough money to buy a hamburger and a cup of coffee?"[71] King also warned that

---

71   King, *All Labor Has Dignity*, 175, from a speech in Memphis on March 18, 1968, to the American Federation of State, County, and Municipal Employees (AFSCME).

the second part of the civil rights movement's fight for freedom would be harder: "It is much more difficult to eradicate slums than it is to integrate a bus."[72] This concern signals important developments in the civil rights movement, as it expanded from questions of personal and political rights to economic rights. While mainline politicians have picked up King's question to argue for the need to create more economic equality,[73] Hill Collins's notion of the matrix of domination and our analysis of class and production push for a deeper understanding not only of the challenges of the capitalist economic system but also of the intersectionality of race, gender, and class.

A deepened understanding of domination and exploitation along the lines of class can throw some light on a deeper understanding of domination along the lines of race and gender as well. The shallowest critiques of racism and sexism match the shallow notion of "classism," limited to matters of prejudice and stereotypes. Even self-declared "systemic" critiques of racism and sexism often assume that we are merely dealing with layered forms of prejudice that can somehow be "dismantled" through antiracism and antisexism trainings. To use the example of racism, a deepened analysis would need to take into account the connection between prejudice and power. Power is what accounts for domination, and prejudice supports it. The flow of power is why the term *racism in*

---

72   Reference in Honey, *To the Promised Land*, 163.

73   Democratic presidential candidate Amy Klobuchar, referenced in Maeve Reston, "Buttigieg Comes under Fire as Democratic Debate Heats Up," *CNN*, December 19, 2019, https://www.abc57.com/news/buttigieg-comes-under-fire-as-democratic-debate -heats-up.

reverse makes little sense. But what powers are at work here? Not only are privilege and power often confused, but prejudice and power are often confused as well.

When trying to understand what kind of power is at work in racism and how it dominates people and robs them of their agency, we need to return once more to our analysis of neoliberal capitalism. Class analysis throws light on the fact that domination and oppression are fundamentally aimed at exploitation. The conditions of North Atlantic chattel slavery and their role in capitalist development show what is at stake: whether slave owners got satisfaction from dominating and oppressing their slaves or not (some certainly did), the main objective of slavery was not domination or oppression as such but the production of profit and prosperity for the owners. A similar observation applies to labor relations under the conditions of capitalism, where domination always serves a purpose: making money for the stockholders. Yet while domination and oppression are fundamentally tied to exploitation, the reality of exploitation is often repressed.

Although it may allow for some concern about domination, oppression, exclusion, and "othering," capitalism and the culture it has created in the academy and in faith communities cannot allow for a succinct analysis of exploitation. Capitalism may also allow for lowering the handicap of certain identities along the lines of race and gender, which is the job of diversity offices and hospitality initiatives, but it needs to uphold the illusion that those who are still not successful when the handicap is lowered are somehow to blame for their misfortune. And while capitalism might allow for the rise to the top of a few minorities or members of the working or middle class, it cannot allow for exposing the exploitative nature of labor relations, let alone for ending them. It is for these reasons that class analysis is necessary for a deeper understanding of the systemic natures of racism and sexism and for addressing them. Put the other way around, without understanding capitalism and labor relations, remedies for racism and sexism tend to fall short, lured into the false promises of nondiscrimination, education, professionalism, self-help, and social ventures.[74] This is one of the problems faced by theology in the Capitalocene as well, especially when it comes to definitions of sin and salvation.

As developed in the previous chapter, class marks relationships of exploitation, extraction, and power. Intersectional analysis can help us see that these relationships are not limited to economic relations but touch on all other relationships, including the ones marked by identities of race, ethnicity, sexuality, gender, and nationality but also those that define religion and interactions with the divine that are at the heart of the study of theology. This is where questions of class and identity are most closely related, and class itself can also be examined as a matter of identity ("class for itself"; see previous chapter). Understanding class as identity produced in the context of dominant power—both as a matter of exploitation and as a matter of resistance and the production and reproduction of alternatives—can in turn also inform the understanding of identity along the lines of

---

74 Nicole Aschoff, *The New Prophets of Capital* (London: Verso, 2015), 92–93. Aschoff describes how Oprah, for instance, fuses identity politics with self-help, the ethics of Horatio Alger, spirituality, and religion (100).

race, ethnicity, gender, sexuality, and nationality. While the constructed nature of all these identities has been the topic of many contemporary theoretical approaches,[75] the topic to be investigated further in conjunction with class analysis is how these identities are produced in relationships that are subject to the flow of power in the Capitalocene.

Understanding class as an identity constructed under outside pressures in a struggle against exploitation might provide lessons for the development of other identities, as this identity is always open ended and subject to transformation and deconstruction when relationships change. If none of our relationships are natural or God-given—including race, ethnicity, gender, sexuality, and nationality—they must therefore be open ended as well. As political scientist Jodi Dean has argued, "Identities are sites of struggle rather than grounds of struggle,"[76] and this has implications for how to embody, develop, and transform identities in the struggles against domination, oppression, and exploitation and how best to put them to use in the production of resistance and positive alternatives.

Black women on the progressive Left have recognized what is at stake here in various ways. Activist, academic, and public intellectual Angela Davis talks about the identity of Black women as a "provisional identity that allows the move beyond identity politics,"[77] leading to new forms

---

75   For the topic of race, see, for instance, what is now commonly known as *critical race theory*. For the topics of gender and sexuality, see the work of Judith Butler and many of the French feminist theorists, like Julia Kristeva and Hélène Cixous.

76   Dean, *Comrade*, 16.

77   Angela Y. Davis, "Reflections on Race, Class, and Gender in the USA," in *The Angela Y. Davis Reader*, ed. Joy James (Malden, MA: Blackwell, 1998), 313.

of solidarity that bring together concerns of race, gender, and class. Identities can be starting points, but they are not where it all ends, an argument that has also been made by Hill Collins and Bilge.[78] Davis recommends to "consider 'women of color' a point of departure rather than a level of organizing."[79] She argues for the formation of coalitions that are grounded not in identity but in political projects, where people resist domination and oppression and tie together not only the usual groups that might be seen as resisting, such as prisoners, immigrant workers, and labor unions; these coalitions also link prisoners and students, students and immigrant workers, and so on.[80] The late professor bell hooks notes the importance of class to identity politics, arguing that "women of all races and black people of both genders are fast filling up the ranks of the poor and disenfranchised. It is in our interest to face the issue of class, to become more conscious, to know better so that we can know how best to struggle for economic justice."[81] In other words, the politics of class and the politics of identity do not have to stand in opposition. The problem is what Briahna Joy Gray has identified as "the cynical weaponizing of identity politics for political ends" in order to "forestall initiatives aimed at economic equality."[82]

---

78 Hill Collins and Bilge, *Intersectionality*, 132: "Understandings of the politics of identity can constitute *a starting point of intersectional inquiry and praxis and not an end in itself*" (emphasis in original). Three forms of identity can be useful: "Identities as strategically essential, identities as de facto coalitions, and transformative identities" (133).

79 Davis, "Reflections," 320. She cautions of the "pitfalls of essentialism."

80 Davis, 324.

81 bell hooks, *Where We Stand: Class Matters* (New York: Routledge, 2000), 8.

82 Gray, "Beware the Race Reductionist."

In each of these examples, there is a class base from which "deep solidarity" can emerge, as the 99 percent who do not belong to the executive class are beginning to understand that they share some things in common despite their differences, starting with their exploitation. Exploited are workers of all races and genders on whose backs the neoliberal capitalist economy is built but also the members of the middle class of all races and genders, who may find it hard to admit that their jobs are increasingly precarious and their retirements in jeopardy and who have to come to terms with the fact that their children can no longer count on moving further up the social ladder than their parents. Theology in the Capitalocene may find not only challenges but also inspirations here.

While in this chapter we have talked mostly about race, feminist and womanist concerns match many of the concerns addressed, since women are always more affected by economic exploitation than men. It is no accident that most of the poor are women—in particular, single mothers. In the theological academy, it is still too often overlooked that (as historian Dorothy Sue Cobble reminds us) strong currents in US feminism were not only closely related to labor issues from the 1920s through the 1960s but also led by women who were engaged in the labor movement.[83] Women shaped the labor movement profoundly, even in unexpected organizations like steelworker unions.[84] The realities of womanism

---

83 Dorothy Sue Cobble, "When Feminism Had Class," in *What's Class Got to Do with It? American Society in the Twenty-First Century*, ed. Michael Zweig (Ithaca, NY: ILR, 2004), 25.

84 Mary Margaret Fonow, *Union Women: Forging Feminism in the United Steelworkers of America*, vol. 17 (Minneapolis: University of Minnesota Press, 2003).

predate Alice Walker's coining of the term. Lucy Parsons, for instance, an African American labor organizer in the late nineteenth and early twentieth centuries, brought together race, gender, and class in her own ways, noting how sex and race "were facts of existence manipulated by employers who sought to justify their greater exploitation of women and people of color."[85] From an Argentinean perspective, social scientist Verónica Gago has argued that "the feminist movement has launched a new critique of political economy" that "includes a radical denunciation of the contemporary operations of capitalism" and provides alternatives via "popular economies, as reproductive and productive webs."[86] On the whole, women's movements have often been much more intersectional than the mainline realized. In the study of religion and theology in particular, it would be worthwhile to reclaim some of the histories of socialist feminisms.[87]

Today, the labor movement in the United States is increasingly led by women, who make up 46 percent of its membership.[88] Journalist Nichole Aschoff has made a strong argument for a "feminism of the 99 percent," concluding that the concerns of feminists and the concerns of progressives on the left converge in the deeper goals of "justice and

---

85 Quoted in Dean, *Comrade*, 38–39.

86 Verónica Gago, *Feminist International: How to Change Everything*, trans. Liz Mason-Deese (London: Verso, 2020), 240.

87 Some of this has already been done in the works of ethicist Beverly Harrison and theologian Dorothee Sölle, but even many of their students have not continued it.

88 Blado, Essrow, and Mishel, "Who Are Today's." See also "Coalition of Labor Union Women: About Cluw," Coalition of Labor Union Women, accessed March 25, 2022, http://www.cluw.org/?zone=%2Funionactive%2Fview_page.cfm&page=About20CLUW; and "Women Innovating Labor Leadership," WILL Empower, accessed March 25, 2022, https://www.willempower.org/.

equality for all people, not simply equal opportunity for women or equal participation by women in an unjust system."[89] Deep solidarity begins with this insight rather than with pious appeals, wishful dreams, or great ideas, which are often confused with religion and theology.

Conclusions

Moving beyond narrow forms of identity and class politics and developing new forms of solidarity opens up new ways of addressing power in terms of residual dualisms—even as dualism has been declared outdated and is therefore often shunned in religious and theological studies. Yet unlike traditional theological and philosophical dualisms located in identities seemingly fixed in nature and metaphysics, many of which can be safely relegated to the history books, we are now dealing with dualisms of raw power to exploit and extract that are constructed and can therefore be deconstructed as well. Just like workers are only workers in relation to their bosses, Black people are Black in relation to whites,[90] whatever is defined as feminine exists in relation to the masculine, gay is defined in relation to straight, and so on. All these identities can now be considered in terms of their construction in relations of power and are therefore open ended and open to revision and reconstruction. Only when this is

---

89 Nicole Aschoff, "Feminism against Capitalism," *Jacobin*, February 29, 2016, https://www.jacobinmag.com/2016/02/aschoff-socialism-feminism-clinton-sandberg-class-race-wage-gap-care-work-labor.

90 See also Victor Anderson, *Beyond Ontological Blackness: An Essay on African American Religious and Cultural Criticism* (London: Bloomsbury, 2016).

seen clearly does resistance become a real option, starting always from particular identities.

The dualism of power in a neoliberal capitalist global world, where the proverbial rich get richer and the poor get poorer, serves as a stark reminder that dualism cannot be erased simply by rejecting the idea of it as outdated and affirming unity. Real resistance to dualisms requires recognizing them, noting their relations to the dualism of the exploitation of human and nonhuman work by the dominant interests of capitalism, and moving forward with this in mind. It may come as a surprise that corporate executives, too, have something to gain in the struggle—namely, an opportunity to switch their allegiances ("conversion" in theological terms) and to embrace nonexploitative and nonextractive relationships with other people, the world, and God.

Whatever class consciousness and related identities develop in this struggle does not perpetuate the naturalized dualisms of narrow identity politics (where race, ethnicity, gender, and sexuality are essentialized and romanticized). In fact, recognizing the constructed nature of dualisms is the first step to overcoming them, with the potential of bringing clarity and resolve not only to the extremes but even to those who are in the middle, where much of the battle is waged—the middle class. These comments are not meant to deny the importance of other more subtle ways of resistance suggested by postcolonial critics and others, like "tactical ambiguity," protective compliance, mimicry, and disguised resistance.[91] There is

---

91 The variety of options is nicely summarized by New Testament scholar Warren Carter and captured in Fernando F. Segovia, "A Postcolonial Commentary on the New

plenty of room for hybridity, mimicry, and ambivalence even in class analysis,[92] but what first initiates resistance may well be a sense of the ever-worsening and death-dealing dualism of class exploitation in the form of the brutal extraction of human and nonhuman resources.

If this is clear, the struggle shifts from what is often considered to be "special interests" or "interest groups" to common interests.[93] The labor unions' motto that "an injury to one is an injury to all" can now be extended beyond the working majority to matters of race, gender, and ecology. Christian theologians might recover a similar insight expressed by the apostle Paul in the midst of Roman exploitation that "if one member suffers, all suffer together with it" (1 Cor 12:26). Of course, the constructed dualisms of race, class, and gender are best seen from the perspective of those who suffer the most from them—from below. From above, dualisms are usually played down, especially by those on top who hold firm to the myths of individualism, as if women, ethnic and racial minorities, and working people were simply keeping themselves down and are thus to blame for their own

Testament Writings," in *A Postcolonial Commentary on the New Testament Writings*, ed. Fernando F. Segovia and R. S. Sugirtharajah (London: T&T Clark, 2009), 32.

92 See, for instance, the essays in a volume on the question of class identity and postmodernity: J. K. Gibson-Graham, Stephen A. Resnick, and Richard D. Wolff, eds., *Re/Presenting Class: Essays in Postmodern Marxism* (Durham, NC: Duke University Press, 2001). These essays emphasize fluid and uncentered understandings of class identity, counter an imagined capitalist totality, and provide new and creative means of resistance. See, for example, 16–21. See also the postmodern reading of class offered by Stephen A. Resnick and Richard D. Wolff, *Knowledge and Class: A Marxian Critique of Political Economy* (Chicago: University of Chicago Press, 1989).

93 See Joerg Rieger, "Developing a Common Interest Theology from the Bottom Up," in *Liberating the Future: God, Mammon, and Theology*, ed. Joerg Rieger (Minneapolis: Augsburg Fortress, 1998), 124–41.

misfortune. The truth, of course, is that the wealth of the few is by and large produced on the backs of the many via human and nonhuman labor, which is why individualism is one of the favorite myths of the dominant class. The same is true for male, white, or heterosexual privilege: it is produced on the backs of others and has to be accounted for, which is why "men must see sexism as *their* problem, white people must see race as *their* issue,"[94] and so on.

In the end, hope not only for people but also for the planet is found in the observation that capital itself is not autonomous but produced and reproduced in social relations and that these relations can be changed because solidarity may be possible after all.[95] Theology in the Capitalocene will have to weigh these arguments in relation to the location of the divine.[96]

---

94 Johnson, *Privilege, Power, and Difference*, 60.
95 See Néstor Míguez, Joerg Rieger, and Jung Mo Sung, *Beyond the Spirit of Empire: Theology and Politics in a New Key* (London: SCM, 2009), chap. 2.
96 For some initial reflections on this matter, see Rieger, *Jesus vs. Caesar*.

Conclusions

Solidarity and Reparations

The Demand for Reparations

I n place of a summary of the arguments presented in this book, I will address one crucial matter that emerges from all the chapters: reparations. In the United States, the conversation about reparations has a specific location in the history of slavery, but the concern for reparations applies more broadly also to everything discussed in this volume, including ecological destruction, class relationships, and the intersectionalities of race, ethnicity, sexuality, and gender, as well as the notion of deep solidarity. For theologians, this is the context in which reflections on confession of sin and repentance, addressed in the previous chapter, need to prove themselves.

On the political scene in the United States, demands for reparations entered a new stage when, on April 14, 2021, the US House Judiciary Committee voted for the creation of a commission to address the matter. H.R. 40, as introduced on January 4, 2021, by Rep. Sheila Jackson Lee[1] (and every

---

1   "H.R.40—Commission to Study and Develop Reparation Proposals for African Americans Act," Congress.gov, January 4, 2021, https://www.congress.gov/bill/117th-congress/house-bill/40.

year since 1989 by Jackson Lee and the late John Conyers) calls for a commission to study and develop reparation proposals for African Americans.

The matter of reparations for the descendants of enslaved African Americans keeps gaining urgency, as the realities of systemic racism were exposed again for all to see in the damage done by the Covid-19 pandemic to the African American community, whose death rate was 1.4 times higher than that of white communities,[2] and in the murders of George Floyd, Breonna Taylor, and many others that have sparked the Black Lives Matter social movement. Strong conservative pushback—no Republicans voted for H.R. 40, and critical race theory is being challenged by conservatives across the board[3]—only demonstrates the potency of the call for reparations, which cannot be ignored indefinitely. Time alone will not be able to heal this wound.

The question sparked by our reflections on deep solidarity in the previous chapter is not whether reparations are in order or not but what kinds of reparations might be most appropriate. Mere apologies for evil done, or simply assuming that the past is past, would hardly be acceptable in any relationship, be it interpersonal, communal, national, or international. Germany recognized this after the

---

2 "The Covid Racial Data Tracker," The COVID Tracking Project, accessed March 25, 2022, https://covidtracking.com/race.

3 Barbara Sprunt, "Understanding the Republican Opposition to Critical Race Theory," NPR, June 20, 2021, https://www.npr.org/2021/06/20/1008449181/understanding -the-republican-opposition-to-critical-race-theory.

Holocaust,[4] even though the process was long and arduous. Many of us who grew up after the war in Germany were raised to understand the importance of reparations and were better for it. From a theological perspective, apologizing or confessing without repentance and transformation would be not only insufficient but counterproductive and ultimately harmful for all involved.

In the United States, powerful arguments for reparations have been made at various times. One of the most prominent examples is the Black Manifesto, presented by civil rights leader James Forman at Riverside Church in New York City in 1969, which specifically addressed white mainline denominations and Jewish communities in order to hold them accountable to their stated mission to care for others.[5] Other examples of calls for reparations include Dr. Martin Luther King Jr.'s proposed 1964 "Bill of Rights for the Disadvantaged" that pointed out the intergenerational nature of sin registered by the prophets of the Hebrew Bible[6] and A. Philip Randolph, Bayard Rustin, and King's 1967 "Freedom Budget for All Americans" that linked racial and

---

4 "Reparations Agreement between Israel and the Federal Republic of Germany," Wikipedia, accessed March 25, 2022, https://en.wikipedia.org/wiki/Reparations_Agreement _between_Israel_and_the_Federal_Republic_of_Germany.

5 Juan Floyd-Thomas, "The God That Never Failed: Black Christian Marxism as Prophetic Call to Action and Hope," in Choi and Rieger, *Faith, Class, and Labor*, 66. See this chapter for a comprehensive account of the importance of the Black Manifesto for faith communities today and on the background of debates about reparations since the US Civil War.

6 Martin Luther King Jr., "We Need an Economic Bill of Rights: An Abridged Version of the Civil Rights Leader's 1968 Essay Published in Look Magazine Shortly after His Assassination," *Guardian*, April 4, 2018, https://www.theguardian.com/commentisfree/ 2018/apr/04/martin-luther-king-jr--economic-bill-of-rights.

economic justice and was endorsed by the Southern Christian Leadership Conference.[7]

A more recent prominent argument to white America for reparations was made by author and journalist Ta-Nehisi Coates in 2014,[8] pointing out the systemic problems of slavery and the kind of racism that remains shackled to it. Coates, referencing historian David W. Blight, notes that in 1860, enslaved people had been turned into assets whose combined worth surpassed America's manufacturing, railroad, and productive capacities. Problems continued even after this atrocity was ended. Even after slavery was abolished in the United States, African Americans were excluded from progress—for instance, from the increase in homeownership from 30 percent in 1930 to 60 percent in 1960. Coates describes the profitable business of redlining, using the example of Chicago. Whites were actively pressured into selling their houses by unscrupulous white businessmen, who spooked them into selling for cheap. These businessmen then sold these houses to Blacks on contract for double the price, making them pay all the costs of housing without actually gaining ownership until everything was paid off, forfeiting the properties altogether if only one payment was missed.

These basic points, narrated by Coates, not only show the structural nature of American racism during and after

---

7 A. Philip Randolph, Bayard Rustin, and Martin Luther King Jr., "A Freedom Budget for All Americans," Poverty & Race Research Action Council (PRRAC), January 1967, https://www.prrac.org/pdf/FreedomBudget.pdf.

8 Ta-Nehisi Coates, "The Case for Reparations," *Atlantic*, June 2014, https://www.theatlantic.com/magazine/archive/2014/06/the-case-for-reparations/361631/.

slavery; they also show how closely racism has always been related to matters of the economy and of class. Based on these observations, an argument can be made that the common definition of racism as "prejudice and power" needs to be expanded to something like "prejudice, power, and capital." As economist and political scientist Jessica Gordon Nembhard argues, drawing the conclusions of her study of the history of African American cooperatives in the United States, "Early on African Americans realized that without economic justice—without economic equality, independence and stability (if not also economic prosperity)—social and political rights were hollow, or actually not achievable." Theologians will be interested to know that religion played a role here as well—Gordon Nembhard references W. E. B. Du Bois's observation that "religious comradery was the basis for Black economic cooperation."[9]

Already in the nineteenth century, twenty African American religious leaders (nineteen of which had been enslaved) recognized this combination of race and class. Their thoughts are recorded in a conversation with General William Tecumseh Sherman, which fed into Sherman's famous campaign for "forty acres and a mule" (immediately abandoned by his successor). In the understanding of these religious leaders, labor is crucial when dealing with reparations. According to their spokesperson, Garrison Frazier, "Slavery is, receiving by *irresistible power* the work of another man, and not by his *consent*. The freedom, as I understand it, promised

---

9 Jessica Gordon Nembhard, "Interventions Forum Co-ops," Wendland-Cook Program in Religion and Justice, October 2020, https://www.religionandjustice.org/interventions -forum-coops. For the full study, see Gordon Nembhard, *Collective Courage*.

by the proclamation, is taking us from under the yoke of bondage, and placing us where we could reap the fruit of our own labor, take care of ourselves and assist the Government in maintaining our freedom." This concern for the ability to labor and have agency underlies the demand for land: "The way we can best take care of ourselves is to have land, and turn it and till it by our own labor—that is, by the labor of the women and children and old men; and we can soon maintain ourselves and have something to spare."[10] Having experienced slavery in their own bodies, the analysis of these leaders is still as relevant as ever. Note that in Native American struggles, labor and community wealth also shape the often-noted concern for land, putting together human and nonhuman productive and reproductive labor, as suggested in chapters 1 and 2.[11]

Deepening the Reparations Debate

The topic of reparations can be deepened in light of these insights: if slavery and racism are so closely related to the economy and money, it follows that reparations need to involve the economy and money. Even religious confessions and repentance for sin have to be embodied in material

---

10 "Newspaper Account of a Meeting between Black Religious Leaders and Union Military Authorities," Freedmen and Southern Society Project, June 2021, http://www.freedmen.umd.edu/savmtg.htm (emphasis in original).

11 See, for instance, Kari Marie Norgaard, Ron Reed, and Carolina Van Horn, "Continuing Legacy: Institutional Racism, Hunger, and Nutritional Justice on the Klamath," in *Cultivating Food Justice: Race, Class, and Sustainability*, ed. Alison Hope Alkon and Julian Agyeman (Cambridge, MA: MIT Press, 2011), 25, talking about "the importance of land for the accumulation of wealth, and its absence for the production of hunger" in a specific Native American community.

relationships, as became clear both during and after slavery. For Coates, this connection between racism, the economy, and money means that reparations should take the form of payments by white America to Black America, similar to the payments that Germany has kept making to Israel for many years. These payments, Coates points out, were fundamental to building the Israeli economy into what it is today (although US support should not be overlooked). What Coates fails to notice, however, is the problematic nature of an economy that was created in this way, as Israel (tied with the United States) has the worst inequality in the developed world.[12] This fundamental economic inequality is made worse by the other inequality that it enables—namely, Israel's sustained and systemic pushback against Palestinian interests, which is often misunderstood as merely some kind of family feud.

On this background, another argument for reparations becomes necessary. This argument has implications for the ongoing exploitation of African Americans in the United States and extends to exploitation everywhere manifest in the lives of the working majority, which embodies human diversity more than any other group or body. Moreover, this argument has implications also for the nonhuman working majority, which experiences the exploitation of its vast and still largely unexplored biodiversity and the systemic extraction of its resources. The argument to be developed here picks up the importance of reparations in monetary

---

12 Alanna Petroff, "U.S. and Israel Have Worst Inequality in the Developed World," *CNN Money*, May 21, 2015, https://money.cnn.com/2015/05/21/news/economy/worst-inequality-countries-oecd/.

and economic terms but suggests another way forward by taking us back to the original distortions and what might be done about them. Theology in the Capitalocene can benefit from these considerations as well.

One of the most significant aspects of slavery—even if not the only one—is a fundamental distortion of labor relations, combining the matters of race and class. As Karen and Barbara Fields point out, this distortion of labor relations under the conditions of slavery was "so abnormal . . . that it required an extraordinary ideological rationale—which then and ever since has gone by the name *race*."[13] As argued in chapter 3, labor and class relations can be considered distorted if one party profits disproportionally at the expense of another; moreover, this distortion affects every other area of life, including religion and theology. A classic example of a distorted labor relation is wage theft. While there is considerable disagreement about the profit employers make from the labor of their employees and about how much is too much and how much is enough, there is little disagreement about wage theft.[14] Even conservatives—conservative religious bodies and theologians included—who rarely worry about employers making too much profit would for the most part agree that wage theft is wrong.

In the context of labor and class relations, slavery amounts to wage theft, a conversation that goes back at least as far as

---

13 Fields and Fields, *Racecraft*, 266–67. The Fields continue, "The initial designation of Afro-Americans as a race on the basis of their class position has colored all subsequent discussion of inequality, even among white persons" (268).

14 David Cooper and Teresa Kroeger, "Employers Steal Billions from Workers' Paychecks Each Year," Economic Policy Institute, May 10, 2017, https://www.epi.org/publication/employers-steal-billions-from-workers-paychecks-each-year/.

Frederick Douglass (see chapter 4).[15] We might even say that slavery is the ultimate wage theft, as what is stolen is not merely wages but everything: lives, relationships to family and community, and sometimes even people's spirits and souls. This is arguably the core problem of the history of slavery in the United States. As this problem is being revisited, it should also be kept in mind that while the legal enslavement of African Americans was officially abolished in the United States in the eighteenth century after the Civil War, slavery continues today in other forms both nationally and internationally. More people from a greater variety of backgrounds are enslaved today than ever before in the history of the world, literally owned by others who exploit them for profit. Worst of all, these enslaved individuals have become more expendable than anyone enslaved in the past.[16] Addressing the history of slavery in the United States will have to have implications for addressing and eradicating contemporary slavery as well.

Keeping in mind the history of slavery, wage theft may be a good starting point for a conversation about reparations today, as it has taken on epidemic proportions in certain industries such as construction and food services. It should give us pause that the value of stolen wages each year is higher than all other theft combined.[17] Most affected are

---

15 As Floyd-Thomas, "God That Never Failed," points out, Douglass's assumption that "his new life as a free man began the first day he received his earned wages" creates other problems, as wage labor implies another relationship of exploitation.

16 Kevin Bales, *Disposable People: New Slavery in the Global Economy* (Berkeley: University of California Press, 2012), notes the awful truth that, compared to today's enslaved people, the African American slaves were "sizeable investments" for their masters.

17 Meixell and Eisenbrey, "Wage Theft."

often undocumented immigrant workers and other minority workers and women. Wage theft is now being addressed by a growing number of worker centers with the goal of returning as many stolen wages as possible. Through these efforts, returning stolen wages might be considered a form of reparations today, serving as one model for past wage theft.

The responsibility for the repayment of stolen wages, including the wages of enslaved people, is on those who pocketed them. Who exactly is responsible for stolen slave wages in the history of the United States will need to be examined, but examples often mentioned include government, NGOs, institutions of higher education, and religious communities.[18] At stake is not just what they once gained but what they continue to gain. Beyond this list, special consideration will need to be given to those whose gains are greatest, above all to the substantial concentration of wealth in corporations and the role of financial capital.[19]

In addition to reparations for the blatant exploitation of labor, there is also the matter of reparations for blatant ecological exploitation and extraction, addressed by womanist ethicist Melanie Harris. Harris notes that "ecological reparations problematize some of the framers of environmentalism, acknowledge the impact of colonial ecology, and replace dualistic understandings that divide the earth from the heavens, for example with a more fluid frame that

---

18 Keri L. Day, "How Princeton Seminary's Slavery Audit Created Moments of Unlikely Intimacy," *Christian Century*, June 10, 2021, https://www.christiancentury.org/article/reflection/how-princeton-seminary-s-slavery-audit-created-moments-unlikely-intimacy.

19 Zoe Thomas, "The Hidden Links between Slavery and Wall Street," *BBC News*, August 29, 2019, https://www.bbc.com/news/business-49476247.

values interconnectedness and interdependence."[20] Harris's comments point to important theological matters such as the relation between heaven and earth and the spiritual and the material. In conversation with these insights, a theology in the Capitalocene needs to develop the theological concerns for interconnectedness and interdependence in relation to the topic of solidarity as it grows out of collective experiences of exploitation and extraction and an analysis of class (see chapter 4).

While theology in the Capitalocene can sometimes embrace mainline solutions, it always needs to move beyond them. Compared to the "three Rs" of established environmentalism (reduce, reuse, recycle), four other "Rs" suggested by environmental sociologist Hannah Holleman are more fundamental: restitution (of land and sovereignty), reparations, restoration, and revolution. These four Rs are connected in that they are all "moving away from capitalism."[21] How might reparations, in particular, aid in moving away from a form of capitalism that is built on the exploitation of people and the planet, and how might theology be part of this?

Reparations and Solidarity

When discussing reparations, who deserves repayment and what form such repayments should take require another look. Beginning with the latter issue, if labor and class relations are

---

20 Melanie L. Harris, *Ecowomanism: African American Women and Earth-Honoring Faiths* (Maryknoll, NY: Orbis Books, 2017), 145.

21 Holleman, *Dust Bowls of Empire*, 162.

at the heart of the problem of both slavery and its aftermath, merely redistributing money does not go far enough. Wage theft may serve as the example: while repaying stolen wages is preferable to withholding them indefinitely, it does not address or change the skewed class relationships (backed by racial, ethnic, and gendered relationships) that enable wage theft in the first place. And even if wage theft were to cease, most relationships of exploitation would continue, as they are backed by perfectly legal labor relationships under the conditions of capitalism, often supported by religious claims and theological arguments.[22] Similar insights can be applied to the problem of extraction of natural resources: ending the most pernicious forms of extraction does not put an end to the exploitation of the nonhuman world in order to create profits for the few rather than the many, one of the foundational principles of capitalism.

This brings us back to the problem of the Capitalocene, in which capitalism shapes not only the economy but also our political, religious, and theological imagination at the deepest levels. Historians have argued that capitalism has taken such severe forms in the United States because of the history of slavery. As enslaved people were exploited in the production of cotton, resources were extracted from the land, whose biodiverse vegetation was cleared for a single crop. Slavery produced an intricate hierarchy of labor, exploitation, and extraction—utilizing numerous middlemen and meticulous bureaucratic control—resulting in enormous wealth for

---

22 For theological support of capitalism, see Michael Novak, *The Spirit of Democratic Capitalism* (New York: Simon & Schuster, 1982).

plantation owners. At the beginning of the Civil War, there were more millionaires in the Mississippi Valley than anywhere else in the United States. The meticulous methods of control over slave labor in the South predated the use of these methods over industrial labor in the North.[23] Based on that history, as historian of religion Juan Floyd-Thomas argues, the United States still finds it difficult to acknowledge the rights of labor because it has never addressed and remedied the problem of enslaved labor.[24] It is not surprising, therefore, that US labor relations continue to be among the most restrictive in the world.[25]

All these observations emphasize the need for reparations that go beyond the quick fix, pointing to another solution that can no longer ignore the reparation of labor relations. In the United States, reparations need to begin with African Americans, whose ancestors have been enslaved and who still experience the aftereffects of these abusive relationships over a century and a half later. If the legacy of relationships of exploitation and extraction would be rectified where they have been most distorted, this would affect other relationships as well and result in a virtuous circle, with implications for other people and the planet.

---

23 "It was not so much the rage of the poor white Southerner but the greed of the rich white planter that drove the lash. The violence was neither arbitrary nor gratuitous. It was rational, capitalistic, all part of the plantation's design." See Princeton historian Matthew Desmond's "In Order to Understand the Brutality of American Capitalism, You Have to Start on the Plantation," *New York Times Magazine*, August 14, 2019, https://www.nytimes.com/interactive/2019/08/14/magazine/slavery-capitalism.html.

24 Floyd-Thomas, "God That Never Failed," 58.

25 The Protecting the Right to Organize Act of 2021 (PRO Act) before Congress may remedy some of this, but there is no denying that the United States is far behind other developed countries and that it would take a long time to catch up.

Reparations that transform relationships of exploitation and extraction might pick up on, but would also go beyond, the politics of recognition ("I see you," "I hear you") currently in vogue in faith communities and theological circles. Without reparations and the systemic transformation of relationships, such a politics of recognition is too easily co-opted by capitalism, which can also benefit from recognition and diversifying the ranks of its supporters.

In sum, if reparations were tied to the transformation and reversal of exploitative and extractive relations of production and reproduction, several problems could be solved together, with major implications for a theology in the Capitalocene.

Those most severely affected by distorted labor and class relations would find some relief and gain that which matters most: the agency of which slavery and the exploitative labor relations that were devised in its aftermath deprived them. Here, confession of sin and repentance would truly lead to salvation for the many rather than just for the few whom the dominant system mistakenly considers the elect. In the United States, this would benefit African Americans first of all, but it would also benefit immigrants and women, with beneficial consequences for the nonhuman environment. Ongoing racial discrimination, which is part of the live legacy of slavery, could now be addressed where it is often most destructive and painful but often ignored: at work, where people spend the bulk of their waking hours and where the well-being of whole communities is decided not only in the form of wages and benefits but also in the availability or absence of economic democracy. This would have consequences for addressing racial discrimination everywhere, including omnipresent microaggressions. If theology in the Capitalocene fails to pay attention to this, it may not have much of a game, no matter what its theological arguments are and no matter how much it supports a politics of recognition or the matrix of difference (discussed in the previous chapter).

In sum, if labor and class relations would be revised and improved with an eye toward those who are most adversely affected by them, this would have beneficial effects for all who are suffering from distorted labor relations. This is the deep wisdom of the Black Lives Matter movement—namely, that starting with those lives who are most endangered and threatened at present is nonnegotiable if all lives are supposed to matter.[26] Such an approach would ultimately benefit even white working people, who, in the process, could gain the motivation to reexamine their racial prejudices when they learn that they are up against not people of other races or nationalities but something else—the Capitalocene. These insights are backed up by the observation that improving labor relations via unionization tends to have benefits not only for workers within the union itself but for all who work in related areas, decreasing wage gaps and improving the power of working people everywhere.

The basis for all of this is not primarily morality, which is often where theology ends up and gets stuck, but solidarity—not as another moral demand on well-meaning people but as the levelheaded observation of systemic

---

26 This need to lift up Jesus's concern for the "least of these" is also the heart of liberation theology's preferential option for the poor, and this is what those who perpetuate the callous motto that "all lives matter" in opposition to "Black lives matter" overlook.

affinities and common interest. As Touré Reed has pointed out, while Coates may assume "that moral suasion is the engine of political change, the historical record makes clear that coalitions built on mutual interest . . . have been essential to blacks' material advancement."[27] The solidarity among working people that emerges from this is not without its complexities, but it is so powerful because it is built on shared interests (self-interest is not selfishness, chapter 4), and it extends to solidarity with the nonhuman environment as well. For theology in the Capitalocene, this means that its work is rooted not primarily in morality but in reconstructed relationships, which are inseparable from a reconstructed relationship with God from which new ethical inspiration can eventually emerge.

Finally, reparations that address labor relations are less prone to fueling other inequalities, like Germany's reparation payments to Israel did. In this model, agency changes hands from elites in business and politics and returns to those whose lives and relationships are most affected—beginning, in the United States, with the majority of descendants of enslaved Africans who continue to struggle. Agency in every other realm can then begin to change hands as well, leading to surprising discoveries of the difference people are able to make in solidarity with one another and the world around them. Networks of worker cooperatives that are

---

27 Reed, *Toward Freedom*. Reed rejects Ta-Nehisi Coates's call for reparations based on "altruistic noblesse oblige." My argument here is that reparations can and need to be based on stronger motivations. Reed concludes his book with the statement that "the fate of poor and working-class African Americans—who are unquestionably overrepresented among neoliberalism's victims—is linked to that of other poor and working-class Americans" (172).

emerging around the globe and that have a long history in African American communities in the United States serve as inspiring examples.[28] To be sure, such solutions will never be devised from the top down; instead, they will have to be promoted and pushed by those with whom the power in a democracy supposedly lies: "we, the People," not only in national but also in international perspective. For theology in the Capitalocene, this means that divine agency will have to be reconsidered as well in these ways, completely transforming what popular civil religion in the Pledge of Allegiance now calls "one nation under God." Perhaps a statement along the lines of "humans and nonhumans cooperating in solidarity with each other and with God" would be more like it.

Religion and theology have a particular role to play in these conversations for various reasons. For starters, religion and theology have been part of the problem of slavery, distorted labor relations, and ecological destruction from the very beginning. Slavery was not only religiously condoned; it was endorsed and promoted.[29] Moreover, all of these distorted relations have always resulted in distorted images of the divine as well, as has been argued throughout this book. God has too often been made to look like the powerful of any age, including white Southern plantation and slave owners of the past and CEOs and politicians of the present, working

---

28 See Gordon Nembhard, *Collective Courage*; "U.S. Federation of Worker Cooperatives—Work It. Own It," US Federation of Worker Cooperatives, accessed March 25, 2022, https://www.usworker.coop/home/.

29 Sydney E. Ahlstrom, *A Religious History of the American People* (New Haven, CT: Yale University Press, 1972), 654, describes how the idea that "slavery was a 'positive good'" gained increasing support in the 1830s.

via relationships of exploitation and extraction. At the same time, however, religion and theology also have been part of the struggle against oppression and exploitation from the beginning, embodied in the lives and theologies of enslaved Africans and their descendants but also in often-forgotten efforts to reshape the interrelated relationships of class, race, and gender in popular religion linked to people's movements at the grass roots.[30] In the process, alternative images of the divine and divine agency have emerged that are at the core of the work of theology resisting and pushing beyond the Capitalocene. That these efforts continue today testifies to powers at work that scholars of theology and religion, and the faith communities to which they relate, ignore at their own peril.

---

[30] See, for instance, the popular images of the historical Jesus emerging in such contexts, which are almost completely forgotten in religious and theological studies; Burns, *Life and Death*.

Acknowledgments

This book sorts, summarizes, and engages questions, challenges, struggles, and solutions that emerged over three decades of teaching in the theological academy and engagement in various social movements. More people would deserve to be mentioned than can be listed here, but I would like to express my profound appreciation to some of my fellow travelers who continue to inspire me, noting that any shortcomings of this text are solely my own.

I am grateful for incisive, critical, and constructive comments on the text of this book by John Aden, Jim Crosby, Obery Hendricks, Don Jones, Filipe Maia, Don Manning Miller, and Santiago Slabodsky. Parts of it were developed in ongoing conversations with colleagues and collaborators around the world, who may not always remember their profound input into my thinking, including Naim Ateek, Whitney Bauman, Philip Clayton, Marcus Briggs Cloud, Kerry Danner, Dennis Dickerson, Wilson Dickinson, Ulrich Duchrow, Timothy Eberhart, Ken Estey, Tripp Fuller, Alois Halbmayr, Jione Havea, Franz Hinkelammert, Jamin Hübner, M. P. Joseph, Catherine Keller, Simangaliso Kumalo, Kwok Pui-lan, Cynthia Moe Lobeda, Néstor Míguez, Jessica Gordon Nembhard, Elaine Nogueira Godsey, Gabriella Lettini, Jeremy Posadas, Michael Ramminger, Claudio

De Oliveira Ribeiro, Annika Rieger (who also contributed to chapter 1), Rosetta Ross, Terra Schwerin Rowe, Sudipta Singh, Jung Mo Sung, Juan Floyd Thomas, George Tinker, Miguel De La Torre, Tim VanMeter, George Zachariah, Upolu Luma Vaai, Karl Villarmea, Cornel West, Gerald West, and Richard Wolff, as well as working groups at the American Academy of Religion (the Class, Religion, and Theology Unit; the New Materialism, Religion, and Planetary Thinking Seminar; and the Energy, Extraction, and Religion Consultation) and the Transdisciplinary Theological Colloquy at Drew University.

The Wendland-Cook Program at Vanderbilt University, which I am directing, has proven to be invaluable for my work. I am grateful to the members of the leadership team, including Aaron Stauffer, Francisco Garcia, and George Schmidt (who also proofread the manuscript and compiled the index); the more than two dozen student fellows who have worked with us over the years; and donor Barbara Wendland and the Cook Foundation. One of the great blessings of Wendland-Cook is academic collaboration. Working with faculty fellows such as Jin Young Choi, Chaumtoli Huq, Charlene Sinclair, and Jeremy Posadas has been an immense privilege and joy. I would also like to express my appreciation to the editors of this series, particularly to Ashley Moyse, with whom I have been in conversation throughout, and to the editorial team of Fortress Press and Will Bergkamp.

Having worked with various labor-related organizations over the years, including the Nashville Central Labor Council led by Vonda McDaniel, I am especially indebted to the work done by the Southeast Center for Cooperative Development in Nashville and its codirectors Benny Overton and Rosemarie Henkel-Rieger. Rosemarie, of course, is also my partner in life, and she has discussed many of the ideas of this book with me over the years, often wondering about the usefulness of theology and religion but always respecting it where it is able to make a difference. The Southeast Center also housed a collaborative inquiry team of academics, activists, and faith leaders, funded by the Louisville Institute, that developed a road map for bringing together religion and worker cooperatives with a focus on emboldening marginalized communities (https://www.co-opsnow.org/tool-kit) that may hold the key to many things discussed in this volume.

Selected Bibliography

Ahlstrom, Sydney E. *A Religious History of the American People*. New Haven, CT: Yale University Press, 1972.

Ahmed, Sara. "Orientations Matter." In Coole and Frost, *New Materialisms*, 248–254.

Allen, Thomas W. *The Invention of the White Race: The Origin of Racial Oppression in Anglo-America*. London: Verso, 1997.

Andersen, Margaret L., and Patricia Hill Collins. "Why Race, Class, and Gender Still Matter." In *Race, Class, and Gender: An Anthology*, edited by Margaret L. Andersen and Patricia Hill Collins, 1–14. Boston: Cengage Learning, 2010.

Anderson, Victor. *Beyond Ontological Blackness: An Essay on African American Religious and Cultural Criticism*. London: Bloomsbury, 2016.

Asad, Talal. *Genealogies of Religion: Discipline and Reasons of Power in Christianity and Islam*. Baltimore: Johns Hopkins University Press, 1993.

Aschoff, Nicole. "Feminism against Capitalism." *Jacobin*, February 29, 2016. https://www.jacobinmag.com/2016/02/aschoff-socialism-feminism-clinton-sandberg-class-race-wage-gap-care-work-labor.

———. *The New Prophets of Capital*. Jacobin. London: Verso, 2015.

Bageant, Joe. *Deer Hunting with Jesus: Dispatches from America's Class War*. Carlton, Australia: Scribe, 2009.

Bales, Kevin. *Blood and Earth: Modern Slavery, Ecocide, and the Secret to Saving the World*. New York: Spiegel & Grau, 2016.

———. *Disposable People: New Slavery in the Global Economy*. Berkeley: University of California Press, 2012.

Barnes, Sara. "Viral Posts Claim Wombats Are Shepherding Animals to Their Burrows during Australian Bushfires." My Modern Met, January 15, 2020. https://mymodernmet.com/viral-wombat-post-australia-bushfires/.

Barth, Karl. *Dogmatics in Outline*. New York: Harper & Row, 1959.

Bauman, Whitney A. *Religion and Ecology: Developing a Planetary Ethic*. New York: Columbia University Press, 2014.

Benjamin, Walter. *Kapitalismus Als Religion*. Edited by Dirk Baecker. 2nd ed. Berlin: Kulturverlag Kadmos, 2004.

Bennett, Lerone. *Before the Mayflower*. New York: Penguin, 1982.

Betancourt, Sofia. "Ethical Implications of Environmental Justice." In *Justice on Earth: People of Faith Working at the Intersections of Race, Class, and the Environment*, edited by Manisha Mishra-Marzetti and Jennifer Nordstrom, 37–45. Boston: Skinner House Books, 2018.

Beverley, John. *Subalternity and Representation: Arguments in Cultural Theory*. Durham, NC: Duke University Press, 2004.

Blado, Kayla, Dan Essrow, and Lawrence Mishel. "Who Are Today's Union Members?" Economic Policy Institute, August 31, 2017. https://www.epi.org/publication/who-are-todays-union-members/.

Bobo, Kim. *Wage Theft in America*. New York: New Press, 2011.

Boff, Leonardo. *Cry of the Earth, Cry of the Poor*. Translated by Philip Berryman. Maryknoll, NY: Orbis Books, 1997.

Bottomore, Tom. *A Dictionary of Marxist Thought*. Oxford: Blackwell, 2006.

Bourdieu, Pierre. *The Social Structures of the Economy*. Translated by Chris Turner. Cambridge: Polity, 2016.

Braidotti, Rosi. "The Politics of 'Life Itself' and New Ways of Dying." In Coole and Frost, *New Materialisms*, 201–220.

Breen, Richard. "Foundations of a Neo-Weberian Class Analysis." In *Approaches to Class Analysis*, edited by Erik Olin Wright, 31–50. Cambridge: Cambridge University Press, 2007.

Burns, David. *The Life and Death of the Radical Historical Jesus*. Religion in America. New York: Oxford University Press, 2013.

Buttel, Frederick H. "Ecological Modernization as Social Theory." *Geoforum* 31, no. 1 (2000): 57–65.

Candeias, Mario. "Eine Frage Der Klasse: Neue Klassenpolitik Als Verbindender Antagonismus." In *Klassentheorie: Vom Making und Remaking*, edited by Mario Candeias, 459–470. Hamburg, Germany: Argument, 2021. https://www.rosalux.de/fileadmin/rls_uploads/pdfs/sonst_publikationen/Candeias_Klassentheorie_gesamt.pdf.

Cannon, Katie G. *Katie's Canon: Womanism and the Soul of the Black Community*. Minneapolis: Fortress, 2021.

Cantwell, Christopher D., Heath W. Carter, and Janine Giordano Drake, eds. *The Pew and the Picket Line: Christianity and the American Working Class*. Working Class in American History. Urbana: University of Illinois Press, 2016.

Chaturvedi, Vinayak, ed. *Mapping Subaltern Studies and the Postcolonial*. London: Verso, 2000.

Chibber, Vivek. *The Class Matrix: Social Theory after the Cultural Turn*. Cambridge, MA: Harvard University Press, 2022.

Christiano, Kevin J., William H. Swatos, and Peter Kivisto. *Sociology of Religion: Contemporary Developments*. 2nd ed. Lanham, MD: Rowman & Littlefield, 2008.

Clark, Brett, and Richard York. "Carbon Metabolism: Global Capitalism, Climate Change, and the Biospheric Rift." *Theory and Society* 34, no. 4 (August 2005): 391–428.

Climate Action 100+. "Climate Action 100+." October 21, 2021. http://www.climateaction100.org.

CLUE. "Clue." Accessed October 27, 2021. https://www.cluejustice.org/.

Coalition of Labor Union Women. "Coalition of Labor Union Women: About Cluw." Accessed March 25, 2022. http://www.cluw.org/?zone=%2Funionactive%2Fview_page.cfm&page=About20CLUW.

Coates, Ta-Nehisi. "The Case for Reparations." *Atlantic*, June 2014. https://www.theatlantic.com/magazine/archive/2014/06/the-case-for-reparations/361631/.

Cobb, John B. "Christianity, Economics, and Ecology." In *Christianity and Ecology: Seeking the Well-Being of Earth and Humans*, edited by Dieter T. Hessel and Rosemary Radford Ruether, 497–511. Cambridge: Center for the Study of World Religions, 2000.

Cobble, Dorothy Sue. "When Feminism Had Class." In *What's Class Got to Do with It? American Society in the Twenty-First Century*, edited by Michael Zweig, 23–34. Ithaca, NY: ILR, 2004.

Commission to Study and Develop Reparation Proposals for African Americans Act. H.R. 40. Congress.gov, January 4, 2021. https://www.congress.gov/bill/117th-congress/house-bill/40.

Cone, James H. *A Black Theology of Liberation*. Maryknoll, NY: Orbis Books, 1970.

Conniff, Richard. *The Natural History of the Rich: A Field Guide*. New York: W. W. Norton, 2003.

Connley, Courtney. "In 1 Year, Women Globally Lost $800 Billion in Income Due to Covid-19, New Report Finds." *CNBC*, April 30, 2021. https://www.cnbc.com/2021/04/30/women-globally-lost-800-billion-dollars-in-income-due-to-covid-19.html.

Cook, John, Naomi Oreskes, Peter T. Doran, William R. L. Anderegg, Bart Verheggen, Ed W. Maibach, J. Stuart Carlton, Stephan Lewandowsky, Andrew G. Skuce, and Sarah A. Green. "Consensus on Consensus: A Synthesis of Consensus Estimates on Human-Caused Global Warming." *Environmental Research Letters* 11, no. 4 (April 13, 2016). https://iopscience.iop.org/article/10.1088/1748-9326/11/4/048002.

Coole, Diana H., and Samantha Frost. "Introducing the New Materialisms." In Coole and Frost, *New Materialisms*, 1–46.
———, eds. *New Materialisms: Ontology, Agency, Politics*. Durham, NC: Duke University Press, 2010.

Cooper, David, and Teresa Kroeger. "Employers Steal Billions from Workers' Paychecks Each Year." Economic Policy Institute, May 10, 2017. https://www.epi.org/publication/employers-steal-billions-from-workers-paychecks-each-year/.

Corbin, Thomas, and J. P. Deranty. "Foucault on the Centrality of Work." OnWork Newsletter, November 2, 2020. https://onwork.substack.com/p/foucault-on-the-centrality-of-work.

Cort, John C. *Christian Socialism: An Informal History*. Maryknoll, NY: Orbis Books, 2020.

The COVID Tracking Project. "The Covid Racial Data Tracker." Accessed March 25, 2022. https://covidtracking .com/race.

Cox, Harvey. *The Market as God*. Cambridge, MA: Harvard University Press, 2016.

Crockett, Clayton. "Plasticity and Change: Rethinking Difference and Identity with Catherine Malabou." In Hughes, Martin, and Padilla, *Ecological Solidarities*, 168–185.

Crockett, Clayton, and Jeffrey Robbins. *Religion, Politics, and the Earth: The New Materialism*. New York: Palgrave Macmillan, 2012.

Daly, Herman E., and John B. Cobb. *For the Common Good: Redirecting the Economy toward Community, the Environment, and a Sustainable Future*. 2nd ed. Boston: Beacon, 1994.

Davis, Angela Y. "Reflections on Race, Class, and Gender in the USA." In *The Angela Y. Davis Reader*, edited by Joy James, 307–325. Malden, MA: Blackwell, 1998.

Day, Keri L. "How Princeton Seminary's Slavery Audit Created Moments of Unlikely Intimacy." *Christian Century*, June 10, 2021. https://www.christiancentury.org/article/reflection/ how-princeton-seminary-s-slavery-audit-created-moments -unlikely-intimacy.

Dayton, Donald W. "'Good News to the Poor': The Methodist Experience after Wesley." In *The Portion of the Poor: Good News to the Poor in the Wesleyan Tradition*, edited by M. Douglas Meeks, 68–96. Nashville: Kingswood Books, 1995.

Dean, Jodi. *Comrade: An Essay on Political Belonging*. New York: Verso, 2019.

Desmond, Matthew. "American Capitalism Is Brutal. You Can Trace That to the Plantation." *New York Times*, August 14,

2019. https://www.nytimes.com/interactive/2019/08/14/magazine/slavery-capitalism.html.

Dorrien, Gary. *American Democratic Socialism: History, Politics, Religion, and Theory*. New Haven, CT: Yale University Press, 2021.

———. *The New Abolition: W. E. B. Du Bois and the Black Social Gospel*. New Haven, CT: Yale University Press, 2015.

Douglass, Frederick. "If There Is No Struggle There Is No Progress." Black Past, 1857. https://www.blackpast.org/african-american-history/1857-frederick-douglass-if-there-no-struggle-there-no-progress/.

———. *My Bondage and My Freedom*. Edited by William L. Andrews. Urbana: University of Illinois Press, 1987.

Draut, Tamara. *Sleeping Giant: How the Working Class Will Transform America*. New York: Doubleday, 2016.

Du Bois, W. E. B. *Black Reconstruction in America: Toward a History of the Part Which Black Folk Played in the Attempt to Reconstruct Democracy in America, 1860–1880*. 1st ed. New York: Free Press, 1965.

———. *Writings by W. E. B. Du Bois in Periodicals Edited by Others*. Vol. 4, collated and edited by Herbert Aptheker. Millwood, NY: Kraus-Thomson Organization, 1982.

Duchrow, Ulrich, Reinhold Bianchi, René Krüger, and Vincenzo Petracca. *Solidarisch Mensch werden: Psychische und soziale Destruktion im Neoliberalismus*. Hamburg: VSA Varlag, 2006.

Duchrow, Ulrich, and Franz Josef Hinkelammert. *Transcending Greedy Money: Interreligious Solidarity for Just Relations*. New Approaches to Religion and Power. New York: Palgrave Macmillan, 2012.

Dunbar, Anthony P. *Against the Grain: Southern Radicals and Prophets, 1929–1959*. Charlottesville: University Press of Virginia, 1981.

Edwards, Jason. "The Materialism of Historical Materialism." In Coole and Frost, *New Materialisms*, 281–298.

Fields, Barbara J., Karen E. Fields, and Daniel Denvir. "Beyond 'Race Relations.'" *Jacobin*, January 17, 2018. https://www.jacobinmag.com/2018/01/racecraft-racism-barbara-karen-fields.

Fields, Karen E., and Barbara J. Fields. *Racecraft: The Soul of Inequality in American Life*. New York: Verso, 2012.

Floyd-Thomas, Juan. "The God That Never Failed: Black Christian Marxism as Prophetic Call to Action and Hope." In *Faith, Class, and Labor: Intersectional Approaches in a Global Context*, edited by Jin Young Choi and Joerg Rieger, 44–68. Intersectionality and Theology Series. Eugene, OR: Pickwick, 2020.

———. "Seeing Red in the Black Church: Marxist Thought and African American Christianity." *Journal of Race, Ethnicity, and Religion* 1, no. 12 (November 2012): 1–46.

Fonow, Mary Margaret. *Union Women: Forging Feminism in the United Steelworkers of America*. Social Movements, Protest and Contention. Vol. 17. Minneapolis: University of Minnesota Press, 2003.

Foster, John Bellamy. *Marx's Ecology: Materialism and Nature*. New York: Monthly Review Press, 2000.

Fraser, Nancy. "From Redistribution to Recognition? Dilemmas of Justice in a 'Post-Socialist' Age." *New Left Review* 212 (July 1, 1995): 68–93.

———. *Justice Interruptus: Critical Reflections on the "Postsocialist" Condition*. London: Routledge, 1996.

Freedmen and Southern Society Project. "Newspaper Account of a Meeting between Black Religious Leaders and Union

Military Authorities." June 2021. http://www.freedmen.umd
.edu/savmtg.htm.

Freese, Elizabeth. "The Christian Right's Main Moral Argument
against Abortion Rights Ignores This Critical Issue: It's
Time to Raise It." *Religion Dispatches*, May 7, 2021. https://
religiondispatches.org/the-christian-rights-main-moral
-argument-against-abortion-rights-completely-ignores-this
-critical-issue-its-time-to-raise-it/.

Gago, Verónica. *Feminist International: How to Change Everything.*
Translated by Liz Mason-Deese. London: Verso, 2020.

Gebara, Ivone. *Longing for Running Water: Ecofeminism and Liberation.*
Minneapolis: Fortress, 1999.

Geertz, Clifford. *The Interpretation of Cultures: Selected Essays.* New
York: Basic Books, 1973.

Gerteis, Joseph, and Mike Savage. "The Salience of Class in
Britain and America: A Comparative Analysis." *British
Journal of Sociology* 49, no. 2 (June 1998): 252–274.

Gibson-Graham, J. K., Stephen A. Resnick, and Richard D.
Wolff, eds. *Re/Presenting Class: Essays in Postmodern Marxism.*
Durham, NC: Duke University Press, 2001.

Gold, Howard R. "Never Mind the 1 Percent. Let's Talk about
the 0.01 Percent." Chicago Booth Review, 2017. https://
review.chicagobooth.edu/economics/2017/article/never
-mind-1-percent-lets-talk-about-001-percent.

Goldberg, Danny. "The Circular Firing Squad Isn't Amusing
Anymore: The Left Is Tearing Itself Apart." *Nation,* July 19,
2017. https://www.thenation.com/article/archive/the
-circular-firing-squad-isnt-amusing-anymore/.

Goodstein, Laurie, and David D. Kirkpatrick. "Conservative
Group Amplifies Voice of Protestant Orthodoxy." *New York*

Times, May 22, 2004. https://www.nytimes.com/2004/05/22/us/conservative-group-amplifies-voice-of-protestant-orthodoxy.html.

Gottwald, Norman K. "Values and Economic Structures." In *Religion and Economic Justice*, edited by Michael Zweig, 53–77. Philadelphia: Temple University Press, 1991.

Gould, Kenneth A., David N. Pellow, and Allan Schnaiberg. *Treadmill of Production: Injustice and Unsustainability in the Global Economy (the Sociological Imagination)*. London: Routledge, 2008.

Graeber, David, and David Wengrow. *The Dawn of Everything: A New History of Humanity*. New York: Farrar, Straus and Giroux, 2021.

Gramsci, Antonio. *Selections from the Prison Notebooks*. Edited by Quintin Hoare. Translated by Geoffrey Nowell-Smith. New York: International, 1971.

Gray, Briahna Joy. "Beware the Race Reductionist." Intercept, August 26, 2018. https://theintercept.com/2018/08/26/beware-the-race-reductionist/.

Griffin, Paul. "Carbon Majors Report 2017." Carbon Majors Database, July 2017. https://cdn.cdp.net/cdp-production/cms/reports/documents/000/002/327/original/Carbon-Majors-Report-2017.pdf?1501833772.

Gutiérrez, Gustavo. "The Limitations of Modern Theology: On a Letter of Dietrich Bonhoeffer." In *The Power of the Poor in History: Selected Writings*, 222–234. Eugene, OR: Wipf & Stock, 2004.

Haider, Asad. *Mistaken Identity: Mass Movements and Racial Ideology*. London: Verso, 2018.

Hallman, David G., and Aruna Gnanadason. "Women, Economy and Ecology." In *Ecotheology: Voices from the South and North*, 179–185. Maryknoll, NY: Orbis Books, 1994.

Hamer, Fannie Lou. "'We're on Our Way,' Speech before a Mass Meeting Held at the Negro Baptist School in Indianola, Mississippi." Voices of Democracy, September 1964. https://voicesofdemocracy.umd.edu/hamer-were-on-our-way-speech-text/.

Haney López, Ian. *Merge Left: Fusing Race and Class, Winning Elections, and Saving America*. New York: New Press, 2019.

Harding, Sandra G. "Introduction: Beyond Postcolonial Theory; Two Undertheorized Perspectives on Science and Technology." In *The Postcolonial Science and Technology Studies Reader*, edited by Sandra G. Harding, 1–33. Durham, NC: Duke University Press, 2011.

Hardt, Michael, and Antonio Negri. *Empire*. Cambridge, MA: Harvard University Press, 2000.

Hartley, Daniel. "Anthropocene, Capitalocene, and the Problem of Culture." In *Anthropocene or Capitalocene? Nature, History, and the Crisis of Capitalism*, edited by Jason W. Moore, 154–165. Kairos. Oakland, CA: PM, 2016.

Herzog, Frederick. "Theology of Liberation." *Continuum* 7, no. 4 (1970): 515–524.

Hill Collins, Patricia, and Sirma Bilge. *Intersectionality*. Key Concepts. Cambridge: Polity, 1985.

Hilty, Lorenz M., and Thomas F. Ruddy. "Sustainable Development and ICT Interpreted in a Natural Science Context." *Information, Communication & Society* 13, no. 1 (February 2010): 7–22. https://doi.org/10.1080/13691180903322805.

Holleman, Hannah. *Dust Bowls of Empire: Imperialism, Environmental Politics, and the Injustice of "Green" Capitalism*. New Haven, CT: Yale University Press, 2018.

Honey, Michael K. *To the Promised Land: Martin Luther King and the Fight for Economic Justice*. New York: W. W. Norton, 2019.

hooks, bell. *Where We Stand: Class Matters*. New York: Routledge, 2000.

Horsley, Richard A. *Jesus and the Powers: Conflict, Covenant, and the Hope of the Poor*. Minneapolis: Fortress, 2011.

Hughes, Krista E., Dhawn Martin, and Elaine Padilla, eds. *Ecological Solidarities: Mobilizing Faith and Justice for an Entangled World*. University Park: Pennsylvania State University Press, 2019.

Hunsinger, George, ed. *Karl Barth and Radical Politics*. Philadelphia: Westminster, 1976.

Intergovernmental Panel on Climate Change. "Summary for Policymakers: The Science of Climate Change—IPCC Working Group." IPCC Second Assessment: Climate Change, 1995. 18–24. https://doi.org/10.1017/cbo9781107415416.001.

Interreligious Network for Worker Solidarity. Accessed October 27, 2021. https://in4ws.org/.

Isasi-Díaz, Ada María. "Lo Cotidiano: A Key Element of Mujerista Theology." *Journal of Hispanic/Latino Theology* 10, no. 1 (August 2002): 5–17.

———. *Mujerista Theology: A Theology for the Twenty-First Century*. Maryknoll, NY: Orbis Books, 1996.

Jaffe, Dennis. "From Shareholder Primacy to Stakeholder Primacy: How Family Businesses Lead the Way." *Forbes*, March 16, 2021. https://www.forbes.com/sites/dennisjaffe/

2021/02/24/from-shareholder-primacy-to-stakeholder
-primacy-how-family-businesses-lead-the-way/?sh=
4e8984fa21ed.

Jameson, Fredric. *The Political Unconscious: Narrative as a Socially Symbolic Act*. Ithaca, NY: Cornell University Press, 1981.

Johnson, Allan G. *Privilege, Power, and Difference*. 3rd ed. New York: McGraw Hill Education, 2018.

Kaemingk, Matthew, and Cory B. Willson. *Work and Worship: Reconnecting Our Labor and Liturgy*. Grand Rapids, MI: Baker Academic, 2020.

Kaplan, Juliana, and Andy Kiersz. "American Billionaires Added $2.1 Trillion to Their Fortunes during the Pandemic." Business Insider, October 18, 2021. https://www
.businessinsider.com/american-billionaires-add-21-trillion-to
-fortunes-during-pandemic-2021-10.

Kaur, Valarie. *See No Stranger: A Memoir and Manifesto of Revolutionary Love*. London: Oneworld, 2020.

Kautsky, Karl. *Foundations of Christianity: A Study in Christian Origins*. New York: New York International, 1925.

Kearns, Laurel. "Climate Change." In *Grounding Religion: A Field Guide to the Study of Religion and Ecology*, edited by Whitney Bauman, Richard Bohannon, and Kevin J. O'Brien, 2nd ed., 141–146. New York: Routledge, 2017.

Keller, Catherine, Michael Nausner, and Mayra Rivera, eds. *Postcolonial Theologies: Divinity and Empire*. St. Louis: Chalice, 2012.

Kelley, Robin D. G. "What Did Cedric Robinson Mean by Racial Capitalism?" Boston Review, January 12, 2017. https://
bostonreview.net/race/robin-d-g-kelley-what-did-cedric
-robinson-mean-racial-capitalism.

Kim, Grace Ji-Sun, and Susan M. Shaw. *Intersectional Theology: An Introductory Guide*. Minneapolis: Fortress, 2018.

King, Martin Luther, Jr. *All Labor Has Dignity*. Edited by Michael K. Honey. King Legacy. Boston: Beacon, 2011.

——. "We Need an Economic Bill of Rights: An Abridged Version of the Civil Rights Leader's 1968 Essay Published in Look Magazine Shortly after His Assassination." *Guardian*, April 4, 2018. https://www.theguardian.com/commentisfree/2018/apr/04/martin-luther-king-jr--economic-bill-of-rights.

Klein, Naomi. *The Shock Doctrine: The Rise of Disaster Capitalism*. New York: Picador, 2007.

——. *This Changes Everything: Capitalism vs. the Climate*. New York: Simon & Schuster, 2015.

Knibbe, Kim, and Helena Kupari. "Theorizing Lived Religion: Introduction." *Journal of Contemporary Religion* 35, no. 2 (July 13, 2020): 157–176.

Kruse, Kevin Michael. *One Nation under God: How Corporate America Invented Christian America*. New York: Basic Books, 2015.

Kwok Pui-lan. *Postcolonial Imagination and Feminist Theology*. Louisville, KY: Westminster John Knox, 2005.

Kwok Pui-lan and Joerg Rieger. *Occupy Religion: Theology of the Multitude*. Harrisburg, PA: Rowman & Littlefield, 2012.

Lacan, Jacques. "The Function and Field of Speech and Language in Psychoanalysis." In *Écrits: A Selection*, 31–106. New York: W. W. Norton, 1977.

Lafer, Gordon, and Lola Loustaunau. "Fear at Work: An Inside Account of How Employers Threaten, Intimidate, and Harass Workers to Stop Them from Exercising Their Right to Collective Bargaining." Economic Policy Institute, July 23,

2020. https://www.epi.org/publication/fear-at-work-how
-employers-scare-workers-out-of-unionizing/.

Langlois, Shawn. "Rich Get Richer? Here's the Math."
MarketWatch, November 30, 2020. https://www
.marketwatch.com/story/rich-get-richer-heres-the-math
-11606755825.

Leonhardt, David. "College for the Masses." *New York Times*,
April 24, 2015. https://www.nytimes.com/2015/04/26/
upshot/college-for-the-masses.html.

Leonhardt, David, and Stuart A. Thompson. "How Working-
Class Life Is Killing Americans, in Charts." *New York Times*,
March 6, 2020. https://www.nytimes.com/interactive/
2020/03/06/opinion/working-class-death-rate.html.

Liu, Catherine. *Virtue Hoarders: The Case against the Professional
Managerial Class*. Minneapolis: University of Minnesota
Press, 2021.

Lorenz, Chris. "Representations of Identity: Ethnicity, Race,
Class, Gender and Religion; An Introduction to Conceptual
History." In *The Contested Nation: Ethnicity, Class, Religion, and
Gender in National Histories*, edited by Stefan Berger and Chris
Lorenz, 47–48. New York: Palgrave Macmillan, 2008.

Maia, Filipe. *Trading Futures: Toward a Theological Critique of
Financialized Capitalism*. Durham, NC: Duke University Press,
2022.

Mandela, Nelson. "Nelson Mandela: Inaugural Address." WSU
.edu. Accessed October 26, 2021. http://wsu.edu:8080/
~wldciv/world_civ_reader/world_civ_reader_2/mandela
.html.

Martey, Emmanuel. *African Theology: Inculturation or Liberation*.
Maryknoll, NY: Orbis Books, 1993.

Marx, Karl. "Address of the International Working Men's Association to Abraham Lincoln, President of the United States of America." Marx's letter to Abraham Lincoln. International Workingmen's Association 1864, November 7, 1865. https://www.marxists.org/archive/marx/iwma/documents/1864/lincoln-letter.htm.

———. *Capital: A Critique of Political Economy*. Edited by Frederick Engels. Translated by Samuel Moore and Edward Aveling. 1st ed. English ed. Vol. 1. Moscow: Progress, 1887.

———. *Capital: A Critique of Political Economy*. Translated by David Fernbach. 3rd ed. Vol. 3. London: Penguin Classics, 1981.

———. *A Critique of Political Economy*. Translated by Ben Fowkes. Vol. 1 of *Capital*. London: Penguin Classics, 1976.

———. "Eighteenth Brumaire (Sect. VII)." Reference in Bottomore, *Dictionary of Marxist Thought*, 85.

———. *Karl Marx on America and the Civil War*. Translated by Saul K. Padover. New York: McGraw Hill, 1972.

———. *The Poverty of Philosophy*. Translated by H. Quelch. London: Twentieth Century, 1900.

Masuzawa, Tomoko. *The Invention of World Religions: Or, How European Universalism Was Preserved in the Language of Pluralism*. Chicago: University of Chicago Press, 2005.

McBrien, Justin. "Accumulating Extinction: Planetary Catastrophism in the Necrocene." In Moore, *Anthropocene or Capitalocene?*, 116–137.

McCloud, Sean. *Divine Hierarchies: Class in American Religion and Religious Studies*. Chapel Hill: University of North Carolina Press, 2007.

McCloud, Sean, and William A. Mirola, eds. Introduction to *Religion and Class in America: Culture, History, and Politics*, 1–25.

Vol. 7. International Studies in Religion and Society. Leiden, Netherlands: Brill, 2009.

McFague, Sallie. *The Body of God: An Ecological Theology*. Minneapolis: Fortress, 1993.

———. *Life Abundant: Rethinking Theology and Economy for a Planet in Peril*. Minneapolis: Fortress, 2001.

McKibben, Bill. *Falter: Has the Human Game Begun to Play Itself Out?* New York: Henry Holt, 2019.

Meixell, Brady, and Ross Eisenbrey. "Wage Theft Is a Much Bigger Problem Than Other Forms of Theft—but Workers Remain Mostly Unprotected." Economic Policy Institute, September 18, 2014. https://www.epi.org/publication/wage-theft-bigger-problem-forms-theft-workers/.

Metzl, Jonathan Michel. *Dying of Whiteness: How the Politics of Racial Resentment Is Killing America's Heartland*. New York: Basic Books, 2020.

Míguez, Néstor Oscar, Joerg Rieger, and Jung Mo Sung. *Beyond the Spirit of Empire*. Reclaiming Liberation Theology. London: SCM, 2009.

Milbank, John. *Theology and Social Theory: Beyond Secular Reason*. 2nd ed. Malden, MA: Blackwell, 2006.

Mitloehner, Frank M. "Yes, Eating Meat Affects the Environment, but Cows Are Not Killing the Climate." Conversation, April 29, 2021. https://theconversation.com/yes-eating-meat-affects-the-environment-but-cows-are-not-killing-the-climate-94968.

Moe-Lobeda, Cynthia. "Climate Change as Race Debt, Cass Debt, and Climate Colonialism." In Hughes, Martin, and Padilla, *Ecological Solidarities*, 61–80.

Mol, Arthur P. J., and Gert Spaargaren. "Ecological Modernisation Theory in Debate: A Review." *Environmental Politics* 9, no. 1 (2000): 17–49.

Moore, Jason W. Introduction to Moore, *Anthropocene or Capitalocene?*, 1–12.

———. "The Rise of Cheap Nature." In Moore, *Anthropocene or Capitalocene?*, 78–115.

The Mudflower Collective, Katie G. Cannon, Beverly W. Harrison, Carter Heyward, Ada María Isasi-Díaz, Bess B. Johnson, Mary D. Pellauer, and Nancy D. Richardson. *God's Fierce Whimsy: Christian Feminism and Theological Education.* New York: Pilgrim, 1985.

Nelson, Robert H. *Economics as Religion: From Samuelson to Chicago and Beyond.* University Park: Pennsylvania State University Press, 2001.

Nembhard, Jessica Gordon. *Collective Courage: A History of African American Cooperative Economic Development and Practice.* University Park: Pennsylvania State University Press, 2014.

Nichols, John. *The S Word: A Short History of an American Tradition . . . Socialism.* New York: Verso, 2015.

Norgaard, Kari Marie, Ron Reed, and Carolina Van Horn. "Continuing Legacy: Institutional Racism, Hunger, and Nutritional Justice on the Klamath." In *Cultivating Food Justice: Race, Class, and Sustainability*, edited by Alison Hope Alkon and Julian Agyeman, 23–46. Food, Health, and the Environment. Cambridge, MA: MIT Press, 2011.

OECD. "Inequality—Poverty Rate—OECD Data." Accessed October 26, 2021. https://data.oecd.org/inequality/poverty -rate.htm.

Osinski, Keegan. *Queering Wesley, Queering the Church*. Eugene, OR: Cascade Books, 2021.

P2P Foundation. "Capitalocene." Accessed October 25, 2021. https://wiki.p2pfoundation.net/Capitalocene.

Patel, Raj, and Jason W. Moore. *A History of the World in Seven Cheap Things: A Guide to Capitalism, Nature, and the Future of the Planet*. Oakland: University of California Press, 2017.

Pehl, Matthew. *The Making of Working-Class Religion*. Working Class in American History. Urbana: University of Illinois Press, 2016.

Petroff, Alanna. "U.S. and Israel Have Worst Inequality in the Developed World." *CNN Money*, May 21, 2015. https://money.cnn.com/2015/05/21/news/economy/worst-inequality-countries-oecd/.

Poling, James N. *Understanding Male Violence: Pastoral Care Issues*. St. Louis: Chalice, 2003.

Popkin, Gabriel. "'Wood Wide Web'—the Underground Network of Microbes That Connects Trees—Mapped for First Time." Science, May 15, 2019. https://www.science.org/content/article/wood-wide-web-underground-network-microbes-connects-trees-mapped-first-time.

Posadas, Jeremy. "The Invisible Feet of the Market." Institute for Christian Socialism, March 8, 2021. https://christiansocialism.com/invisible-feet/.

Qureshi, Zia. "Tackling the Inequality Pandemic: Is There a Cure?" Brookings, November 17, 2020. https://www.brookings.edu/research/tackling-the-inequality-pandemic-is-there-a-cure/.

Rahman, Grace. "Are 100 Companies Causing 71% of Carbon Emissions?" Full Fact, November 1, 2018. https://

fullfact.org/news/are-100-companies-causing-71-carbon
-emissions/.

Ran, Brant. "How Much Old Growth Forest Remains in
the US?—the Understory." Rainforest Action Network,
November 11, 2008. https://www.ran.org/the-understory/
how_much_old_growth_forest_remains_in_the_us/.

Randolph, A. Philip, Bayard Rustin, and Martin Luther King Jr.
"A Freedom Budget for All Americans." Poverty & Race
Research Action Council (PRRAC), January 1967. https://
www.prrac.org/pdf/FreedomBudget.pdf.

Reed, Adolph. *Class Notes: Posing as Politics and Other Thoughts on the
American Scene*. New York: New Press, 2001.

Reed, Touré F. *Toward Freedom: The Case against Race Reductionism*.
Jacobin. New York: Verso, 2020.

Rehmann, Jan. "Poverty and Poor People's Agency in High-Tech
Capitalism." In Rieger, *Religion, Theology, and Class*,
143–156.

Reich, Michael. "The Economics of Racism." In *The Capitalist
System: A Radical Analysis of American Society*, edited by Richard C.
Edwards, Michael Reich, and Thomas E. Weisskopf,
chap. 10.3. Englewood Cliffs, NJ: Prentice Hall, 1986.

Resnick, Stephen A., and Richard D. Wolff. *Knowledge and Class:
A Marxian Critique of Political Economy*. Chicago: University of
Chicago Press, 1989.

Reston, Maeve. "Buttigieg Comes under Fire as Democratic
Debate Heats Up." *CNN*, December 19, 2019. https://www
.abc57.com/news/buttigieg-comes-under-fire-as-democratic
-debate-heats-up.

Rieger, Joerg. *Christ & Empire: From Paul to Postcolonial Times*.
Minneapolis: Fortress, 2007.

———. "Developing a Common Interest Theology from the Bottom Up." In *Liberating the Future: God, Mammon, and Theology*, edited by Joerg Rieger, 124–141. Minneapolis: Augsburg Fortress, 1998.

———. "Engaging Whiteness (More) Constructively: Conversations with James Cone and Frederick Herzog on the Future of Race and Class in Theology." *Review and Expositor* 117, no. 1 (2020): 58–71.

———. *Jesus vs. Caesar: For People Tired of Serving the Wrong God.* Nashville: Abingdon, 2018.

———. "Liberating God-Talk: Postcolonialism and the Challenge of the Margins." In Keller, Nausner, and Rivera, *Postcolonial Theologies*, 211–214.

———, ed. *No Religion but Social Religion: Liberating Wesleyan Theology.* Nashville: Wesley's Foundery Books, 2018.

———. *No Rising Tide: Theology, Economics, and the Future.* Minneapolis: Fortress, 2009.

———. "Occupy Wall Street and Everything Else: Lessons for the Study and Praxis of Religion." *Peace Studies Journal* 5, no. 1 (January 2012): 33–45. http://peacestudiesjournal.org/volume-5-issue-1-2012/.

———. "Reenvisioning Ecotheology and the Divine from the Margins." *Ecotheology* 9, no. 1 (April 2004): 65–85.

———, ed. *Religion, Theology, and Class: Fresh Engagements after Long Silence.* New Approaches to Religion and Power. New York: Palgrave Macmillan, 2013.

———. "Why Movements Matter Most: Rethinking the New Materialism for Religion and Theology." In Rieger and Waggoner, *Religious Experience and New Materialism*, 135–156.

Rieger, Joerg, and Rosemarie Henkel-Rieger. *Unified We Are a Force: How Faith and Labor Can Overcome America's Inequalities*. St. Louis: Chalice, 2016.

Rieger, Joerg, and Annika Rieger. "Working with Environmental Economists." In *T&T Clark Handbook of Christian Theology and Climate Change*, edited by E. M. Conradie and Hilda P. Koster, 53–64. London: Bloomsbury T&T Clark, 2020.

Rieger, Joerg, and Edward Waggoner, eds. *Religious Experience and New Materialism: Movement Matters*. Radical Theologies and Philosophies. New York: Palgrave Macmillan, 2016.

Robinson, Cedric J. *Black Marxism: The Making of the Black Radical Tradition*. Chapel Hill: University of North Carolina Press, 2000.

Rogers-Vaughn, Bruce. *Caring for Souls in a Neoliberal Age*. New Approaches to Religion and Power. London: Palgrave Macmillan, 2017.

Rowe, Terra Schwerin. *Toward a Better Worldliness: Ecology, Economy, and the Protestant Tradition*. Minneapolis: Fortress, 2017.

Russo, John, and Sherry Lee Linkon. "What's New about New Working-Class Studies?" Introduction to *New Working Class Studies*, 1–18. Ithaca, NY: ILR, 2005.

Ryan-Simkins, Kelsey, and Elaine Nogueira-Godsey. "Tangible Actions toward Solidarity: An Ecofeminist Analysis of Women's Participation in Food Justice." In *Valuing Lives, Healing Earth: Religion, Gender, and Life on Earth*, edited by Lilian Dube, Teresia Hinga, Sarah E. Robinson-Bertoni, and Theresa A. Yugar, 203–222. Vol. 3. ESWTR Studies in Religion. Leuven, Belgium: Peeters, 2021.

Saito, Kohei. *Karl Marx's Ecosocialism: Capital, Nature, and the Unfinished Critique of Political Economy*. New York: Monthly Review Press, 2017.

Sample, Tex. *Hard Living People & Mainstream Christians*. Nashville: Abingdon, 1993.

Schleiermacher, Friedrich. *The Christian Faith*. Edited by H. R. Mackintosh and J. S. Stewart. Edinburgh: T&T Clark, 1986.

Schnabel, Claus. "Trade Unions in Europe: Dinosaurs on the Verge of Extinction?" VoxEU. Centre for Economic Policy Research, November 18, 2013. https://voxeu.org/article/trade-unions-europe.

Schnaiberg, Allan. *The Environment: From Surplus to Scarcity*. New York: Oxford University Press, 1980.

———. "Sustainable Development and the Treadmill of Production." In *The Politics of Sustainable Development: Theory, Policy and Practice within the European Union*, edited by Susan Baker, Maria Kousis, Dick Richardson, and Stephen Young, 71–88. London: Routledge, 1997.

Schnaiberg, Allan, David N. Pellow, and Adam Weinberg. "The Treadmill of Production and the Environmental State." In *The Environmental State under Pressure*, edited by Arthur P. J. Mol and Fredrick H. Buttel, 15–32. Vol. 10. New York: JAI Press, 2002.

Schor, Juliet B. *Plenitude: The New Economics of True Wealth*. New York: Penguin, 2010.

Schor, Juliet B., and Craig J. Thompson. "Cooperative Networks, Participatory Markets, and Rhizomatic Resistance: Situating Plenitude within Contemporary Political Economy Debates." In Schor and Thompson, *Sustainable Lifestyles*, 233–249.

————, eds. *Sustainable Lifestyles and the Quest for Plenitude: Case Studies of the New Economy*. New Haven, CT: Yale University Press, 2014.

Schumacher, Ernst F. *Small Is Beautiful: Economics as If People Mattered*. New York: Harper & Row, 1973.

Schweitzer, Albert. *Civilization and Ethics*. Translated by John Naish. London: A. & C. Black, 1923.

Segovia, Fernando F. "Configurations, Approaches, Findings, Stances." Introduction to *A Postcolonial Commentary on the New Testament Writings*, edited by Fernando F. Segovia and R. S. Sugirtharajah, 1–68. Bible and Postcolonialism. London: T&T Clark, 2009.

Sharlet, Jeff. *The Family: The Secret Fundamentalism at the Heart of American Power*. New York: Harper Perennial, 2009.

Simon, Ruth. "Covid-19's Toll on U.S. Business? 200,000 Extra Closures in Pandemic's First Year." *Wall Street Journal*, April 16, 2021. https://www.wsj.com/articles/covid-19s-toll-on-u-s-business-200-000-extra-closures-in-pandemics-first-year-11618580619.

Simonis, Udo Ernst. "Ecological Modernization of Industrial Society: Three Strategic Elements." In *Economy and Ecology: Towards Sustainable Development*, edited by Franco Archibugi and Peter Nijkam, 119–137. Dordrecht: Springer, 1989.

Singh, Devin. *Divine Currency: The Theological Power of Money in the West*. Cultural Memory in the Present. Stanford, CA: Stanford University Press, 2018.

Sinyai, Clayton. "Mission-Driven Union Busting." *Commonweal*, September 17, 2012. https://www.commonwealmagazine.org/mission-driven-union-busting.

Smith, Adam. *Inquiry into the Nature and Causes of the Wealth of Nations*. Edited with an introduction and notes by Andrew Skinner. New York: Penguin, 1999.

Smith, Sharon. "Race, Class, and 'Whiteness Theory.'" *International Socialist Review* 46 (2006). https://isreview.org/issues/46/whiteness/.

Solnit, Rebecca. "Big Oil Coined 'Carbon Footprints' to Blame Us for Their Greed: Keep Them on the Hook." *Guardian*, August 23, 2021. https://www.theguardian.com/commentisfree/2021/aug/23/big-oil-coined-carbon-footprints-to-blame-us-for-their-greed-keep-them-on-the-hook.

Spaargaren, Gert, and Arthur P. J. Mol. "Sociology, Environment, and Modernity: Ecological Modernization as a Theory of Social Change." *Society & Natural Resources* 5, no. 4 (1992): 323–344.

Sprunt, Barbara. "Understanding the Republican Opposition to Critical Race Theory." NPR, June 20, 2021. https://www.npr.org/2021/06/20/1008449181/understanding-the-republican-opposition-to-critical-race-theory.

Standing, Guy. *The Precariat: The New Dangerous Class*. London: Bloomsbury, 2011.

Stein, Ben. "In Class Warfare, Guess Which Class Is Winning." *New York Times*, November 26, 2006. https://www.nytimes.com/2006/11/26/business/yourmoney/26every.html.

Sung, Jung Mo. *Desire, Market, and Religion: Horizons of Hope in Complex Societies*. New York: Palgrave Macmillan, 2011.

Tabb, William K. Introduction to *Churches in Struggle: Liberation Theologies and Social Change in North America*, edited by William K. Tabb, xvi–xvii. New York: Monthly Review, 1986.

Tanner, Kathryn. *Christianity and the New Spirit of Capitalism*. New Haven, CT: Yale University Press, 2019.

Taylor, Keeanga-Yamahtta. *From #Blacklivesmatter to Black Liberation*. Chicago: Haymarket Books, 2016.

Therborn, Göran. "An Agenda for Class Analysis." *Catalyst* 3, no. 3 (2019): 89–113.

Tillich, Paul. *Systematic Theology*. Vol. 1. Chicago: University of Chicago Press, 1951.

Torres, Sergio, and John Eagleson, eds. *Theology in the Americas*. Maryknoll, NY: Orbis Books, 1976.

Truth in Accounting. "Answers in Animation: What Is the Difference between Millions, Billions, and Trillions?" August 7, 2019. YouTube video, https://www.youtube.com/watch?v=Om3FmWtf2AY.

United Methodist Church. "Our Social Creed." June 27, 2019. https://www.umc.org/en/content/our-social-creed.

United Nations—Sustainable Development Goals. "UN Report: Nature's Dangerous Decline 'Unprecedented'; Species Extinction Rates 'Accelerating.'" Accessed October 23, 2021. https://www.un.org/sustainabledevelopment/blog/2019/05/nature-decline-unprecedented-report/.

US Federation of Worker Cooperatives. "U.S. Federation of Worker Cooperatives—Work It. Own It." Accessed March 25, 2022. https://www.usworker.coop/home/.

Villarmea, Karl James E. "Transcendence in the Time of Neoliberalism: A Theological Reflection on the Employer-Employee Relationship and the Theological Struggle for Everyday Life." In Choi and Rieger, *Faith, Class, and Labor*, 234–260.

Volf, Miroslav. *Work in the Spirit: Toward a Theology of Work*. Eugene, OR: Wipf & Stock, 2001.

Waters, Brent. *Just Capitalism: A Christian Ethic of Economic Globalization*. Louisville, KY: Westminster John Knox, 2016.

Weeks, Kathy. *The Problem with Work: Feminism, Marxism, Antiwork Politics, and Postwork Imaginaries*. Durham, NC: Duke University Press, 2011.

Weininger, Elliot B. "Foundations of Pierre Bourdieu's Class Analysis." In Wright, *Approaches to Class Analysis*, 82–118.

Wendland-Cook Program in Religion and Justice. "History of Social Gospel Personalities at VDS." Accessed October 29, 2021. https://www.religionandjustice.org/social-gospel.

———. "Interventions Forum Co-ops." October 2020. https://www.religionandjustice.org/interventions-forum-coops.

White, Lynn. "The Historical Roots of Our Ecologic Crisis." *Science* 155, no. 3767 (March 10, 1967): 1203–1207. https://www.science.org/doi/10.1126/science.155.3767.1203.

White, Monica M. *Freedom Farmers: Agricultural Resistance and the Black Freedom Movement*. Chapel Hill: University of North Carolina Press, 2021.

Wikipedia. "Reparations Agreement between Israel and the Federal Republic of Germany." Accessed March 25, 2022. https://en.wikipedia.org/wiki/Reparations_Agreement_between_Israel_and_the_Federal_Republic_of_Germany.

WILL Empower. "Women Innovating Labor Leadership." Accessed March 25, 2022. https://www.willempower.org/.

Williams, Delores S. *Sisters in the Wilderness: The Challenge of Womanist God-Talk*. Maryknoll, NY: Orbis Books, 2013.

Williams, Joan C. *White Working Class: Overcoming Class Cluelessness in America*. Boston: Harvard Business Review Press, 2017.

Wolff, Richard D. *Democracy at Work: A Cure for Capitalism*. Chicago: Haymarket Books, 2012.

———. "Religion and Class." In Rieger, *Religion, Theology, and Class*, 27–42.

World Economic Forum. "The Global Social Mobility Report 2020: Equality, Opportunity and a New Economic Imperative." January 2020. https://www3.weforum.org/docs/Global_Social_Mobility_Report.pdf.

Wright, Erik Olin. "Foundations of a Neo-Marxist Class Analysis." In Wright, *Approaches to Class Analysis*, 4–30.

York, Richard. "The Treadmill of (Diversifying) Production." *Organization & Environment* 17, no. 3 (2004): 355–362.

York, Richard, and Eugene A. Rosa. "Key Challenges to Ecological Modernization Theory." *Organization & Environment* 16, no. 3 (September 1, 2003): 273–288.

Zachariah, George. *Alternatives Unincorporated: Earth Ethics from the Grassroots*. Cross Cultural Theologies. London: Equinox, 2011.

Zweig, Michael. "Economics and Liberation Theology." In Zweig, *Religion and Economic Justice*, 3–52.

———. *The Working Class Majority: America's Best Kept Secret*. Ithaca, NY: Cornell University Press, 2012.

Index